MW01227525

A Craft, a Calling and a Cause

Life in the Glory Years of Advertising

By Bill Lane

Bill Lane
A Craft, a Calling and a Cause: Life in the Glory Years of Advertising/Bill Lane
Includes index
ISBN-13: 978-1500664930
1. J. Walter Thompson Company. 2. Photographic industry –
United States. Automobile industry – United States. Telephone
Industry – United States.
TXu 1-812-328
May 26, 2012

Book design by Sven Mohr

To Dede, who saw me through, and to
Don, Dave, Matt and Kate, who carry on.

In advertising, there are long hours
filled with changes and stress. It takes stamina to
bounce back after disappointments and
to be able to attack the problem with fresh energy.
Resilience, the ability to come back,
is basic to success in all parts of the business.
A daunting list of qualities, but the people
who rise to the top have most of them – plus one other…
They have fire in the belly.

David Ogilvy
Confessions of an Advertising Man

Table of Contents

Introduction

Part I

Part II

Whether it is a farmer arriving from a small town in Mississippi to escape the indignity of being observed by her neighbors, or a boy arriving from the Corn Belt with a manuscript in his suitcase and a pain in his heart, it makes no difference: each embraces New York with the intense excitement of first love, each absorbs New York with the fresh eyes of an adventurer...

E.B. White,
Here Is New York

I

Introduction:

I met New York City in June 1967 when advertising was in full throat. It was an exciting place and a worthy way to make both a living and a difference. Gathering the millions under mass media's tent had ceased to be regarded as hucksterism. Indeed, the notion of advertising as a "profession" had taken firm footing, and the people who practiced it well were duly celebrated.

The possibilities for a young copywriter were limitless. If you wrote a jingle that struck the right note, you could find yourself climbing the pop charts. If you turned a vivid phrase, your words often insinuated their way into dinner-party conversation. Dress up the truth in wit and wisdom and people in great numbers would rush out to buy a car named after an insect. Along the way, you rubbed elbows and egos with corporate CEOs one day, and movie stars, famous athletes and recording artists the next. You made up the rules as you went along. It was great fun.

Advertising in the glory days was more than a business; it was show business; a game played on its toes. It had box office and box scores – just like Broadway and baseball. It was woven into the fabric of water-cooler culture. One part entertainment and one part behavioral psychology, it owed a great debt to the audacity of door-to-door salesmanship. It intruded, astounded, seduced or amused, then left the audience with an emotional urge to buy.

The making of advertising in the 1960s was a craft, a calling and a cause -- and New York City was its beating heart. Those brash enough to believe they had the stuff to play on the big stage came from as far away as, ohmahgod, Seattle, Washington. Success was not determined by consumer testing, but decided on the field of play. It was the ultimate in natural selection. The brave and talented were rewarded and promoted. The timid and the dull were found out and sent home. Dozens of upstart, creatively driven agencies -- most notably Doyle Dane & Bernbach – emerged to challenge the old boy, blue suit firms such as J. Walter Thompson. These new agencies didn't exist merely to do their clients' bidding, as traditional agencies were wont to do. They comported themselves as equals and believed in the intrinsic value of their creative ideas. The story is told of Bill Bernbach -- resolutely standing his ground in the face of a client's stern reprimand. Robert Townsend, CEO of Avis, had told Bernbach that Avis could afford only a fraction of what market leader Hertz was spending in advertising. For that smaller dollar, he challenged DDB to create a campaign that would deliver equal impact. "Very well," said Bernbach. "On one condition: You must promise to run exactly what I bring you."

What Bernbach brought him was a primitive looking black and white layout with two fingers making a "V" sign and a modest headline: "Avis is only No.2 in rent a cars. So why go with us?" The other shoe dropped with the first line of body copy "We try harder." Townsend was appalled at the ad's lack of slick visuals and its acknowledgment of being "only No.2" and refused to run it.

III

He was displeased when Bernbach reminded him of his promise.

"Don't forget, Mr. Bernbach, this is my company."

"And don't forget, Mr. Townsend," Bernbach said, "this is my work."

In 1967, evidence of advertising's pervasive presence was everywhere. There were as many music jingle houses in Manhattan then as there are Starbucks coffee houses now. Advertising songs were made like hit records -- at big studios with big orchestras of thirty and more players. No synthesizers, no sir.

Around town, emerging commercial film production companies were breeding directors who would shoot a package of Coke commercials one week and head west the next to begin filming a major motion picture. Sometimes, the commercials gained the director greater currency. At the Academy Awards during the late 60s and into the 70s, Kodak was the primary sponsor of the national telecast. Commercials were shown in the auditorium even as they were being broadcast across America. On more than one occasion, Hollywood's elite rose in applause after a Kodak two-minute song spot. Take a bow, Michael Cimino, Fred Levinson and Stu Hagmann.

So there I stood that day in June at the 10th floor reception desk in the old Graybar Building on the first of what would be my almost 10,000 days at the J. Walter Thompson Company.
They were tumultuous days that began in the uproar of the war-torn 60s, ran through Detroit at the height of the first great American auto crisis, and continued into San Francisco during the birth of the personal computer revolution. They raged through the 90s, when corporate raiders from abroad captured the largest, most

IV

successful American agencies – including J. Walter Thompson --
and altered the nature of the advertising business forever – if not
for the better.

As time traveled, bold marketing-driven companies gave
way to numbers-crunching, shareholder-focused, risk-aversive,
bottom-line bureaucracies. Relationships between agencies and
clients, which once had been built on mutual respect and partnership, dissolved into puddles of distrust. At most big companies,
advertising ceased to be regarded as an investment. Instead, it was
considered a cost, like toilet paper or the light bill. By dramatically reducing agency compensation – and thereby service and involvement – corporate America came to believe that it could save
its way to profit.

But, it wasn't always so.

"Let me call, Mr. Mygatt," the receptionist said and offered
a seat to an overly excited, fairly frightened young man wearing
his only good suit.

"Lane Mr. Bill Lane well here you are and we've been
waiting for you and come come through here yes that's it and we'll
get you started." Phil Mygatt, a bald, round hurricane of a man,
spoke without punctuation. As head of JWT's creative personnel
department, he wielded absolute power of purse and sword, alter-
nately inspiring and frightening his charges from first paycheck to
last. Mygatt had a finely tuned sense for picking up hallway rumors and restroom scuttlebutt. If you got yourself sideways with a
client or a boss, you would find yourself sitting on a sofa in Mygatt's office beneath an odd painting of a boy balancing an egg on
his finger to receive an equal dose of pep talk and tough love.

It was unwise to get on Mygatt's wrong side. A copywriter named Randy Grotzinger once made an impassioned plea for a raise -- to no good result. In an inspired but unwise moment, Randy had a sack of chickenfeed delivered to Mygatt's office. Mygatt was not amused. Grotzinger was fired.

"You must get through the first day folderol papers to fill out medical payroll and all that," Mygatt spit out, "but this very minute I must take you to where you're going to be doing great things which is Group Seven very exciting very exciting and you must meet a very great man come now come now."

Part I

1
Of Consuelo and the Dancing Man

Mygatt opened the door to a dancing man. "SID! SID!" he shouted. The sound of Tommy Dorsey was booming through a stereo system. "This is BILL LANE and he is very bright and he is starting today and he's going to be a star a STAR and you've got him and BILL this is SID OLSEN and it's going to be GREAT and I've got to go now got to go good luck."

Sid Olsen had been soft shoeing when we walked in and continued to soft shoe during Mygatt's impassioned outburst. He could dance, carry on a conversation and read *Women's Wear Daily* (which he was doing at the moment) all at the very same time. "Well, hello to you ...Bill, is it? Good, good. We'll be starting soon. Make yourself at home." He turned again to the *Women's Wear Daily*. One, two, three, four, slide, two, three, four.

We were, Sid and I, strangers in a very large room, paneled floor to ceiling in mirrors, which made the room seem all that much larger. The furniture was a cliché for hip, modern advertising agency, which in 1967 J. Walter Thompson decidedly was not. The pinkish couches with purple polka dots were Thompson's way of raising its skirts above the knee to affect the boutique style of the hot creative shops popping up all over New York City as fast as you could say Jack Tinker. For an agency such as Thompson, whose ideal employee was a Brooks Brothers 44 long from Darien, this was very brave indeed.

One by one, the members of what I would grow to know as Group Seven joined me in the Big Mirror Room. There was not a Brooks Brother in the bunch. The copy chief was Ann Foster, who began calling herself Ann "Tolstoy" Foster to remind one and all that she was bred from good writing stock and took to speaking in an accent that all but eliminated the letter "r" ("mahvelous"). We had a full-time researcher named Mary O'Gorman, who came with her own history: her father was Jonathan Wainwright, U.S. commanding general on the Bataan Death March. The senior art director was Kent Hansen, politely referred to in those days as "flamboyant." Marilyn Landis was a psychologist by training, who specialized in handwriting analysis. Apparently, we had a need for that. Tiu Frankfort was Sid's ever-faithful assistant, whose main job, as close as I could figure, was to make Sid's daily lunch reservation. (Art director Tommy Marchin and I calculated that Sid spent more for lunch during a year than we earned – the both of us.)

The music stopped and so did Sid. That was a signal for the day to begin and for Group Seven to gather around a large glass table to read Consuelo's horoscope from the *New York Daily News*. Since I was the new kid, it was my privilege to read aloud those signs that applied to Group Seven. I could barely muster enough spit to speak, but I did and that got us to a discussion of what the Group was going to do that day. I was to discover that, although Sid was much in demand on Ford and other major agency assignments, as a group we didn't have any permanent accounts. Our job was to try to win new business and, when all others had failed, to help the agency keep an account that was one foot out the door.

I was assigned an office with an art director named Norman Todhunter, who evidently spent his time designing stamps for the United States Post Office and doing very little else.

"Are you starting today?" he asked me as I was trying out my first corporate chair. When I allowed that I was, he said: "What a coincidence. I was just fired." Gulp.

Sidney A. Olson had a patrician's bearing, a reporter's curiosity and a showman's flair. He had "chased Germans all over Europe" during World War II as a correspondent for *Life* and joined J. Walter Thompson in the mid-50s upon creating a groundbreaking communications campaign for Ford called "The American Road." He was known around the New York office as a big thinker, a notion honored there. It was Sid who coined the name "Instamatic" for Kodak's seminal 1960s point-and-shoot camera.

As leader and muse of Group Seven, Sid conferred on us a certain sense of "being" -- not exactly entitlement, but well on its way there. Even though we had no clients currently in commercial production, Group Seven strutted into JWT's screening room B every afternoon at 3:00 to review the latest directors' reels. We went as a group to the movies in mid-day, one time sitting through "The Graduate" twice -- straight through -- because we sensed something new and wonderful was going on. "Notice how Mike Nichols is pre-lapping the sound from the next scene by starting it in the previous one," Sid pointed out. " We may be able to use that."

Tiu managed to secure tickets for every important fashion

4

show and so we went, not fully understanding what was happening, but soaking it all in and learning before anyone else that, next fall, burgundy would be the new black. To this day, my regular reading diet includes *Vogue* and *Harper's Bazaar*. Sid was right. Fashion is where you find the keenest creative eyes, with the truest sense of where the culture is going. Advice to all young copywriters and art directors: don't just pay attention to what your audiences are watching and listening to. Look at what they're wearing.

It was a bully time to be young and in advertising in New York City. The aroma of creativity was seductive and everywhere. Warhol's Factory was just down the street at Union Square and Avedon's studio a few blocks north on East 75th. You could walk west to the Algonquin Round Table, where the ghosts of Robert Benchley and Dorothy Parker presided, or take a cab uptown to Elaine's, where the new journalism ate and drank. You could still spot Dylan in the Village and Alan Ginsburg on the Lower East Side.

As members of Group Seven, we were encouraged to take it all in. The fact that we were idle much of the time made it easy to escape the office. Sid encountered Tommy Marchin and me one afternoon as we wandered in about 4:00. "Ah, now. And where might you have been?" We confessed that we'd spent lunchtime at the Museum of Modern Art and then gone to see "Blow Up." "Good, good," said Sid, turning his back on us and disappearing into his office. "Good, good."

But for all its electricity, New York could be a tough town to make the day through. I shared a third floor walkup on the pregentrified Upper West Side with three fellow JWT poverty-stricken recruits. Notable among them was Steve Darland, who would be a friend and colleague long into my life. Our block, flanked by Columbus and Amsterdam Avenues, had Needle Park at one end and a whorehouse at the other. Our landlord died on his downstairs apartment floor and remained there for a week until Mrs. Gianquinto came to grips with her loss and asked for help. "Steve," she said. "I don't think Mr. Gianquinto is feeling well." Before calling the appropriate authorities, Steve picked up Mr. Gianquinto and gently laid him in his bed.

It took me two subways to get to work, which was okay when the transit workers weren't on strike, which they were for a good stretch of my first year. It was normal to see garbage piled on the sidewalks in the morning. The garbage was generally gone by evening -- if the sanitation workers didn't walk off the job, which they did for nine days in the swelter of my first sticky New York summer.

Even the City's most famous tourist destinations had rough edges and sad underbellies. If you walked by Jack Dempsey's restaurant near 42nd Street, you'd see the old champ sitting vacant-eyed in the window. He'd wave back at you if you waved at him. Across the street and up the block, the open door of the Metropole pulsed with the rhythms of Gene Krupa, playing out his days in a strip joint. Some would argue that the moral reforms of Mayor Giuliani and the slick wholesomeness of Disney have made Times Square a kinder, gentler place. But, to those of us who were there in the dirty old 60s, Broadway was at its lusty best when there were beer-and-shot bars on every block, a three-card-monte scam around the next corner, flotsam outside the St. James Theater and pickpockets in the crowd.

It was hard to keep your belly full on $6,500 a year. But with young teeth and brass balls, you could stretch a dollar. There was a place called Tad's Steakhouse in the heart of the theater district where an ample piece of meat (tasty, though it required an aerobic chew), a large hunk of French bread and a salad cost $1.69. And Darland and I spent many a night perfecting the fine art of Convention Crashing. Almost every evening, there was a gathering of, say, the National Association of Proctologists at the Biltmore or the Roosevelt. "We're sorry," we'd say, "but we can't seem to find our name badges." With apologies, replacement badges would be created right on the spot. By having enough moxie to talk tractors to Iowa corn farmers or hog futures to the National Grange, it's amazing how many shrimp and canapés we could consume in an hour and how many glasses of white wine we could wash them down with.

We really didn't do much work in Group Seven during my few short months there. I didn't learn a whole lot about the practice of doing everyday advertising. But my world was wider, my appetite was whet and my senses were closer to the surface than they'd ever been.

Early in 1968, as we gathered around the usual table to read Consuelo and decide where Sid was to have lunch, the conversation took a different course. "I got a call last night," Sid began. "Group Seven is being disbanded. I guess we'll all be going to different groups now." I suspect Sid had not done a lot of dancing that day.

2

The University of Advertising

It wasn't until I left the isolated world of Group Seven and entered the mainstream of JWT life that I began to fully appreciate the great orchestra that was J. Walter Thompson. There might be a creative revolution raging up and down Madison Avenue. The town might be buzzing about new-wave agencies winning Clios and Gold Pencils. But, oblivious to hype and noise, Thompson marched to its own quiet rhythm – a strong, sure-going beat that played to history rather than to the annual awards season.

In 1868, James Walter Thompson began as a clerk for Carlton and Smith, which acted as an advertising broker for religious magazines. Ten years later, he came up with $500.00 for the business, $800.00 for the furniture, and bought the firm from Carlton. Not without vanity, he renamed it after himself. He made his mark by shifting the company's emphasis from specialty magazines to general women's publications, and by century's end, Thompson had a stranglehold on almost every major woman's magazine in America.

On occasion, J. Walter took to wearing yachting clothes, and answered to the rank of "Commodore." (The oil painting that hangs in headquarters shows him that way.) By reputation, he didn't have a keen sense of humor. So, when considering the following story, we probably have to add our own laugh track. As told, Mr.

Thompson found himself on the Third Avenue El next to a man lugging around a sandwich board.

"What's your business?" the fellow with the sandwich board asked.

"I am an advertising man," said the sober Thompson.

"Why, so am I. Ain't it hell when the wind blows!"

There was no general consensus of what exactly qualified as advertising in those days. Not even serious practitioners had a firm fix on its future. (Actually, early 20th century British newspaper magnate, Lord Northcliffe, gave it a go: "News is what somebody somewhere wants to suppress; all the rest is advertising.") But over time – through pluck, innovation and global foresight – J. Walter Thompson and his spiritual heirs helped draw the outline, fill in the spaces and grow JWT into the largest advertising enterprise in the world. It moved far beyond the narrow definition of "space agency" to establish the concepts of "full service" and "account management." It pioneered the methods by which media were bought – from magazines, of course, but also through the 25 years that radio ruled and on into the formative days of television. It became famous enough for its market research to inspire a cartoon in The New Yorker. "Good morning, Madam," said a well-dressed man to a woman at her doorstep. "J. Walter Thompson would like to know if you are happily married."

During the 1920s and 30s, Thompson opened offices in every region of the free world, propelled by the leadership of Stanley Resor (who had bought the company from J. Walter in 1917 for $500,000) and guided by the field generalship of Sam Meek. JWT became so internationally ubiquitous that it was rumored to have served as a front for the OSS during World War II and for the CIA long after.

New York's "flagship" office (thank you, Commodore) had been situated in midtown Manhattan's Graybar Building since 1926. By the late 60s, it was a marvel of ritual and civility, dignified by fine art in the corridors and in the offices of senior managers. It had its own staff curator -- the imperious Dione Guffey -- who decked the halls with Chagalls and Miros. The furniture was chosen with an eye for antique and period. On the 11th floor, sitting in simple splendor, was the New England Room, which had been transported from a home of revolutionary times, dismantled carefully plank by plank, and reassembled lovingly high above Lexington Avenue. The Executive Dining Room was right next door, where, in a nod to the times, Thompson women who had achieved the station of vice president could join their male counterparts for lunch – but only on Wednesdays. (Around the office, these women were identified by the hats they wore – indoors and at all times – to distinguish them from mere secretaries and junior female copywriters.) After hours, the dining room was transformed into the Meeting Club, with bartenders Timmy and Mario, dressed in tuxedos, serving cocktails to agency professionals, visiting clients and top management alike.

There may have been Mad Men things going on, but they were made considerably less likely due to the efforts of Helen Landsdowne Resor – quite a copywriter in her day – who served the cause of the J. Walter Thompson Company for fifty years at the side of her husband. In a moment of puritanical fervor, Mrs. Resor took it upon herself to order that the solid outer walls of Thompson executive offices be replaced by open grillwork. The effect, if not her overtly stated intent, was to make it that much more difficult to exercise one's libido during working hours or to pour a stiff drink in the middle of the day.

When I began at the agency, Norman Strouse – a man who I could never imagine dancing – was chief executive. I was truly afraid of Mr. Strouse and would duck into the nearest empty office if I saw him coming my way. His manner suggested that it was likely his children called him "Mr. Strouse," too.

He was soon succeeded by Dan Seymour, and the agency took on a certain glow of star power. Imagine: our CEO had played the role of the newscaster in Orson Welles' famous "War of the Worlds" radio broadcast – the one that had people jumping off the Brooklyn Bridge. Alas, Mr. Seymour took a tumble in our estimation when he gave a rousing speech for employees at the old Commodore Hotel about contemporary culture. At a key moment, and with a dramatic flourish, he invoked the name of Bob "Dielan." (Ann Tolstoy Foster had written the speech, and, upon hearing that glorious mispronunciation and the accompanying nervous laughter, she slipped sullenly from the room.)

At about this time, the stature of the Thompson Company almost resulted in a rare misstep. Around the corner from the Graybar, a distinctive new skyscraper was rising, and JWT was invited to become its core tenant. Though the blood rushed and initial agreements had been reached, Seymour and his management team wisely concluded that it would be unseemly to elevate the Company profile above those of its clients. So, Seymour picked up the phone and called Juan Tripp, then chief executive officer of

Pan Am. That's how, on the spine of Park Avenue, the J. Walter Thompson Building became the Pan Am Building.

(J. Walter himself never suffered from such discretion. In the July 8, 1905 edition of the New York Sun, a feature story posed a question and provided the answer: "Does anybody know the size of the biggest sign in New York? ... It's at the corner of Twenty-third street and Fourth avenue and it's 175 feet long. It is the sign of the J. Walter Thompson Advertising Agency.)

For good reason, JWT had come to be known in the industry as the "University of Advertising." Those of us who took to its teaching learned lessons that served well a lifetime. Thompson had lore and wisdom and passed them down from one generation to the next. Early in our creative careers, we were introduced to the words of James Webb Young, JWT's first creative star. He was responsible for a small volume of advertising advice called "A Technique for Producing Ideas" which rings as true today as it did when he wrote it in the 1940s.

Young professionals were mentored and watched carefully, as aspiring ballplayers are studied by scouts. In time, the best and the brightest of us – not just from New York, but from around the JWT world – were posted to far-flung outposts such as Noordvijk, Holland and Delavan, Wisconsin to be battle tested in the company of our peers. As we advanced from JWT office to JWT office – often from country to country -- we took that teaching with us, as well as the friendships we had formed, finding like minds and kindred spirits wherever we went. It was the Thompson Way.

The development of such a culture was made possible by the nature of how agencies earned their pay. Those were the days of the 15% commission, and it says here that no system employed since has equaled its ability to serve the best interests of all parties concerned. Fifteen percent had a balanced way of ensuring that a client would receive full service, and that an agency had the where-withal to staff appropriately, pay top professionals fair market value and train young people to one day assume senior roles. No one is sure who did the original math, but he sure got it right.

There must be angels -- or divine creatures of some sort -- who deliver those they hold in favor to good circumstance. For, upon leaving Group Seven, I was assigned to the Kodak group.

3
The Stars Align

The more than 1,500 souls that populated JWT/New York in 1967 were divided into six separate but equal groups, each with its own account management, media, research, traffic, and creative capabilities. They were individually identified by the name of their largest account or by that of their creative leader, and in-evitably took on the character of both. While the groups orbited in the same solar system, they were on decidedly different planets. It's likely that, if I'd landed anywhere else but on Kodak, I would have lived out my working life as a damn good insurance salesman.

Arnold Grisman and Andy Nelson ran the Ford group. They had neither the time nor inclination to train and mentor young writers and art directors. You were thrown into their churning maw and thrown out without regret or regard. Page Proctor and Bernie Owett ran the high fashion and personal products group and populated it with young people who breathed the latest, hippest air. I was behind that curve.

Looking back, the Siebert group might have worked out. Bill Siebert had Liggett & Myers cigarettes, the United States Marine Corps and a rascal's sense of humor. But the group's advertising all kind of came out sounding like Bill. There didn't seem to be a whole lot of room to find one's own voice. Larry Daloise and the Lever Brothers group would have been a disaster for me. They lived in the hard-core world of package goods, where you wrote to a client-dictated formula (the "Lever Jolt" must happen at exactly 13 seconds into the spot) and where your commercials were tested and re-tested until they were drained of all blood.

Thompson's hotshot creative group of the moment was defined by the Pan Am account and Warren Pfaff. Though Warren had gathered others around him for amusement, this was really a one-man show. Warren wrote the copy, composed the jingles ("Pan Am Makes the Going Great"), produced the television commercials and emptied the wastebaskets at night. I would have had to change my name to "anonymous."

Luckily, I was dispatched to Kodak and taken under the kindly wing of Granger Tripp. Had this been Hollywood, Granger would have been Jimmy Stewart. He was tall and laconic and presided over us all with an equanimity that belied the rough and tumble that typified creative departments. I never once heard Granger raise his voice. Yet he inspired fierce loyalty and demon-

14

strated daily how you could control wild horses with a gentle rein.

Eastman Kodak was then regarded as among the premiere manufacturing and marketing companies in the world and one of its most coveted advertising accounts. In the 1880s, George Eastman invented roll film and the first point-and-shoot cameras, innovations that transformed popular culture in the 20th century. J. Walter Thompson himself placed the original ad for Kodak cameras in 1888 ("You press the button, we do the rest") and JWT had served as Kodak's agency partner off and on since then. Together, they not only collaborated on some mighty fine print advertising, they pioneered the way people watched television in the post-war world.

Examples dazzle. In television's early days, agencies and their clients had a difficult time coming to grips with just how to use the medium's unique combination of sight, sound and motion. Almost without exception, commercials were produced one at a time and broadcast live, often with unintentionally hilarious results. It was primarily through the efforts of Gerry Zornow (who went on to become Kodak chairman) and marketing man Ted Geonek that a new day of television advertising dawned. Why not, they asked, make it general practice to film television commercials the same way Hollywood films movies? That way, advertisers and their agencies would be able to draw on the full palette of motion-picture techniques – location, action, music, effects, voice over narration. Quality would be assured and advertisers could run the commercials over and over again.

They used their own company as a highly visible test case and their agency – J. Walter Thompson – as a partner in crime.

Thompson led the way through the 50s and 60s in producing Kodak commercials that demonstrated the latest filmmaking techniques and stretched the medium in ways that excited attention and invited imitation.

Since the lion's share of motion-picture film was manufactured by Kodak, Zornow and Geonek -- with that one brilliant stroke -- had generated a profitable new revenue stream for their company, shown the way to advertisers and their agencies on how to best use this new medium, and given rise to an industry dedicated exclusively to advertising commercial production.

JWT and Kodak also played a key role in moving one of the post-war's major chicken-and-egg marketing stalemates off dead center. Until the mid-fifties, TV networks produced practically all of their programs in black and white because there were only a very few color television sets in use. In a parallel universe, manufacturers were loath to produce color television sets in any number because most of the network programs were broadcast in black and white.

It took a meeting among Thompson media professionals, Kodak marketing executives and Walt Disney to break the impasse. If Walt would agree to produce his hugely popular "Disneyland" program in color, Kodak would agree to a major extended sponsorship. (It was no coincidence that "Disneyland" was renamed "Walt Disney's Wonderful World of Color.") The deal spurred TV manufacturers – particularly RCA – into making and marketing the first widely available color television sets. Led by NBC, but followed in short order by the other networks, almost all programming (and, not incidentally, commercials) would eventually be produced on color film, manufactured by Kodak.

The marriage of the new technology, Hollywood and advertising came to full expression in Kodak's unprecedented and long-running sponsorship of the Academy Awards. Every spring, JWT would create from 12 to 16 original commercials to run on the telecast. Premiering before the year's largest television audience, this was the direct, if non-football, ancestor to today's annual Super Bowl of advertising.

But creating Kodak television commercials was far in my future. I was assigned to the Kodak group's editorial department. My boss was "print supervisor" Arthur Richmond, his title betraying the reality of old creative ways still practiced at JWT. At one time, print was king at Kodak. A curious man named Reo Young presided over the Kodak advertising department in Rochester, in full denial that this thing called television merited the slightest bit of his attention. Reo had odd ideas. He ordered that 50% of Kodak ads appear on the left-facing page (which ran counter to the prevailing wisdom) because "half the people read magazines backwards."

Arthur Richmond was Reo's man at Thompson and, true to the code, Arthur never strayed from the printed page. Broadcast was left to a separate group of writers, headed by Granger Tripp and included Alan Anderson, son of the playwright Maxwell Anderson, and Ken Thoren.

Writers and art directors didn't work as teams at JWT as they did at the new-wave agencies. We barely knew each other enough to say "hello" in the halls. Arthur would have a meeting with his writers and say he needed headlines for a projector ad. A rather vacant man called Guy LeRoux, distinguished by perpetually dirty eyeglasses and cigarette ashes on his lapels, would give us details and a deadline. I'd bring my headlines to Art and he would circle one or two and have traffic march them down to the art department with instructions to "do up a few layouts." If Kodak approved one of my headlines, I would be asked to write, say, 150 words of copy. It wasn't until traffic – usually in the person of blustery old Henry Turner -- brought it to me days later for proofreading and a signature that I actually saw the ad for the first time.

For the next year, I toiled at the bottom of the Kodak creative food chain. I wrote small space black-and-white ads for camera enthusiast magazines. I wrote seven-word captions for the giant Colorama in Grand Central Station. I wrote local live radio commercials ("Hey, Cleveland, it's the 4th of July. Don't forget to pick up the Kodak film"). I even wrote the customer advice sheets packaged inside every Kodak film box ("For best results, stand with your back to the sun").

The chance to do a television commercial seemed a million miles away. If Granger put word out on a Friday afternoon that he needed ideas for, say, a 30-second Instamatic camera spot, he would have a dozen scripts on his desk by Monday morning – written by the designated TV team. I would beg and borrow those scripts from Granger so I could study and learn. The really good scripts had a sense of rhythm and a distinctive way of setting a scene. There was pace and plot and a telling message at the end. I talked someone in Thompson's AV department into teaching me to thread a Kodak 16mm movie projector, a skill that would serve me well in the not too distant future. I would wait until everybody else had gone home for the night, and then commandeer the Kodak conference room to screen reels of archive spots. When to make a cut. How to use a dissolve. ("A dissolve is a defeat," Sid had said to me. But the skilled writers in the Kodak group could make a dissolve dance.)

Though I was never asked to submit television ideas of my own, I took to doing so anyway. I would work late, often over the weekend, and slip my scripts onto Granger's desk along with everybody else's. Decisions were made far beyond my earshot, and, inevitably, the day would be won by Granger, Alan, Ken and the rest of the television team.

"Bill, did you write this?" It was Alan Anderson at my desk. I confessed that I had. "Well, you just made the cut for the Academy Awards." Wow. I had written a parody version of "Nice 'n' Easy," an old Alan Bergman lyric, and set it against a one-minute story of young love on a summer's day -- captured by a Kodak Instamatic Camera. I was in television! I'd never been to a shoot or attended a music session or heard an announcer read my copy. I had a lot to look forward to. It was a defining day.

When I got home that night, I found a letter waiting for me on the dining room table.

4
Someone Pulls a String

The Sword of Damocles had been hanging over my head since I left the University of Washington, proud owner of a diploma, but suddenly stripped of my student deferment. Many of my contemporaries enrolled in graduate school, signed up for the Peace Corps or crossed the border into Canada to avoid the draft and the Vietnam War. But when I received an offer to join J. Walter Thompson in New York, I threw good sense to the wind and went off to seek my fame and fortune for the princely wage of $6,500.

I landed in a city seething. Long, tall Mayor John Lindsay seemed to be everywhere, walking a head above teeming crowds on tense summer streets, trying to calm a citizenry wracked by racial unrest and anti-war sentiment. Even so, the worst was yet to come. Martin Luther King and Bobby Kennedy had less than a year to live.

In the heat of the moment, it was impossible to stay on the sidelines and out of the debate. Pretty much everyone in my circle of advertising and media friends became involved in the political ferment. We'd chase our careers by day, and then devote our evenings to cause and advocacy. I volunteered to support Republican Governor Nelson Rockefeller, who was locked in a closely contested race for the Republican presidential nomination, and soon found myself writing speeches and standing in for the governor at local community gatherings. Steve Darland threw his shoulder behind Lindsay in the mayor's seemingly impossible quest for a second term. At evening's end, we'd all meet at McSorley's on 7th Street in the East Village to drink cheap ale and argue politics into wee hours.

Such was the ebb and flow of life when, at the moment of my small television triumph, I received greetings from President Richard M. Nixon, inviting me to spend the next two years in the United States Army. A number of events then occurred – coincidental or otherwise – which bear on the story.

I reported to the Army's induction center at Whitehall Street in lower Manhattan on January 6, 1969. After taking the Army's notorious "you're in if you're breathing" physical, I was dispatched to Ft. Jackson, South Carolina for basic training.

Needless to say, there are few perks in basic training. But one night, our squad was allowed to go to the Day Room to have a near beer and watch the Academy Awards.

Let's Take It Nice and Easy
It's Gonna Be So Easy
For Us to Save Today
We've Simply Got to Make Sure
That We Don't Miss the Picture
Before It Gets Away©

I tried to quiet the room, but how do you tell a bunch of horny, cursing, dogface GIs you want them to shut up for a lousy commercial? So I just sat there, alone in my thoughts, and watched the minute unfold. "I wrote that," I said to my bunkmate Charlie Pappas, who was sitting nearby. "Sure you did," he said. "Sure you did."

Upon graduating from basic training, I expected to be assigned to advanced infantry school, as were most of the newly minted buck privates in my company. But on the final day of basic, I was pulled from the ranks and given orders to report to Ft. Gordon, Georgia to begin training as an "information specialist" at the headquarters of the 3rd Army. I was not to be a grunt after all but a newspaper reporter. Though I was never told why I'd been singled out for this relatively attractive assignment, it just so happened that the Secretary of the Army was Stanley Resor, Jr., son of the man who had led J. Walter Thompson for some fifty years. I suspect a string might have been pulled.

As 1970 dawned, I was ordered to Vietnam, where coincidence and good fortune followed. One of my first assignments – now as a "combat" reporter – was to cover a dust-off mission. In a dust-off, medics fly directly into a firefight to airlift the wounded back to basecamp. I grabbed my notebook, camera and M16 and headed for the staging area where the medics and helicopter crews gathered. That's where I met Warrant Officer Robert Mygatt, son of none other than Phil. Even 8,000 miles away, in the middle of absolutely nowhere, I was touched by the long arm of Mygatt.

It was in Vietnam that I received one of my first -- and certainly most vivid -- lessons in market research. We were taught at Thompson that the reaction of an audience is not solely based on what you show and say, but what the audience sees and hears --

and these may be quite different things indeed. To complicate matters, two audiences may look at the very same message and react in decidedly different ways. Thompson called this phenomenon "stimulus and response."

My lesson learned played out at the Dai Wi officers club in Cu Chi basecamp, where I tended bar for tips. (Lest you get the wrong idea, the "club" was a converted tin-roof hooch with a slat wooden floor, about ten tables and a bar constructed out of empty ammunition cases.) The officers hired me, not for my talents in mixing a martini, but because I knew how to thread a Kodak 16mm movie projector and they were in the habit of watching first-run movies. On one such night, we scheduled the most popular film then running in the United States, acclaimed by critics and audiences alike. After pouring the officers stiff drinks, I switched on the projector and turned off the lights.

There was a gunshot. Everybody hit the deck. We waited a very long moment. I turned on the lights. Amidst the prone bodies scattered about the floor, a captain sat calmly at one table, a pistol in his right hand. He had shot the projector. He had shot *M.A.S.H.* Stimulus and response.

Fortunately, he had not shot me, nor did anyone else. And so, in December 1970, I took a freedom bird back to the real world and J. Walter Thompson.

5
Going Off the Reservation

The 70s would bring enormous change to Kodak and JWT. While the old creative guard was still nominally in place, there was an emerging underclass, impatient with what it considered dated ways, boiling with talent, and itching to run off the leash.

What happened was largely a reflection of the times. The strict moral imperatives that had shaped the so-called "Greatest Generation" had given way to more self-indulgent expression. Conforming had become less important than "doing your own thing." Dress codes were looser, love was freer and the drug culture, which had forever existed on the fringes of society, was now socially mainstream. The youth of the "Sixties Generation" who had spent their formative years in angry resistance against the Vietnam War, in vocal advocacy of women's equality and in fervent protest against racial injustice, was now focusing on the future. It was time for them to move into the work place. And they were bringing their own baggage.

Evidently, my star had risen during the military interlude. Upon returning, I was given a real office instead of a cubicle, a bonus large enough to buy a refrigerator, and Andy Romano. Andy and I were a laboratory experiment: the first art director and copywriter in the New York office to actually sit together and create. No segregated copy department. No isolated art department. Just

Andy and me and our ambition.

"Break the rules," they encouraged us, and we took this as a license to steal. Although there was still a nominal chain of command ("be sure to go through Arthur"), we soon stopped saluting. Slowly, almost imperceptibly, the world began to turn our way. Other young professionals with ideas and ambition appeared around us – not just writers and art directors – but account reps and research planners – even clients. Up there, too, in Rochester, sands were shifting. Budgets had tipped the balance of power from print to television. Roger Morrison and Bruce Wilson had been plucked from JWT's media department to head up Kodak television over Reo Young's sleeping body. And, through some strange gravitational pull, we would all manage to find each other.

Andy and I began to be noticed. A couple of our initial efforts – done for minor Kodak brands – snuck through the system and made the "Ads of the Week" section in *Advertising Age*. This was a relatively rare creative accomplishment for Thompson at the time, still known pejoratively as an "account guy" agency.

But in the Darwinian way these things go, the higher our profile rose, the more we began to meet internal resistance. The old guard, sensing their creative authority slipping away, went into survivor mode. They still controlled the flow of assignments and it was easy to keep the plum ones from Andy and me. Sure, we could play around with ads for Kodak mailers and super 8 movie cameras. But the big game – new-product introductions and the annual Christmas campaign – were kept under territorial lock and key. It was made clear to us that we were still expected to eat at the kids table.

Predictably, it was television that finally broke the old guard's stranglehold. Since my return, I had been asked to do a couple of TV things, based on the success of my first Academy Awards spot. But the old rules still applied. Commercials were ordered up by clients and produced along specific guidelines. Self-generated projects from the agency were not encouraged. Scripts were presented without storyboards ("What do art directors know about television anyway?") Copywriters below the Granger and Alan level neither attended client meetings nor presented their own work. Once a commercial was approved, it was turned over to an agency producer who had not contributed to the concept development nor likely seen the spot before that moment. The copywriter was never involved in pre-production or, heaven forbid, invited to attend the shoot unless there was on-camera dialogue.

I decided to go off the reservation. For my inspiration I looked not to David Ogilvy or Leo Burnett, Carl Ally or Mary Wells, but to a classical music composer from the late 19th and early 20th centuries. When he wasn't involved in one of his many messy affairs, Claude Debussy found time to observe: "Music is the silence between the notes." In the search for my own voice, I began to write that way and came to believe that great advertising is not just clever prose or compelling visuals, but the nuances of meaning and the provocative pauses that inform them – the silence between the notes. In writing a headline or a narrative, I would deliberately leave things out, inviting the viewer to participate in the story, to contribute his or her own personal meaning, to complete the circle.

Not unexpectedly, clients accustomed to seeing a visual

demonstration of key product attributes and trained to expect a detailed exposition of every single copy point were skeptical. I pushed back. "Audiences are used to playing along with film," I would tell them. "Bang! A gun goes off and a bad guy falls. Even though they never see the bullet, viewers readily accept the notion that there was one." I made it my personal creative challenge to never let the audience see the bullet.

It so happened that Warren Aldoretta, a superb agency television producer who had once been an art director, was going through a divorce. He spent many late nights in his office and, though I have no proof, the evidence suggests he may have spent all night there more than once. Because of his innate kindness and creative curiosity, Warren would patiently listen to my ideas and, during his after hours, compose beautiful storyboards to bring them to life. Day after day, I'd write them. Night after night, Warren would draw them. We'd present them to Granger, who always seemed to enjoy the show and then say: "These are great solutions to problems we don't have." The boards piled up against Warren's office wall – ten, twenty, thirty thick.

It was Warren on my phone. "Granger just ran in and grabbed ten of our boards." Kodak was visiting JWT that day for a big television meeting and the agency was dutifully presenting new television spots under the old rules. Evidently, the clients dismissed every one and asked with some frustration: "Don't you guys ever show us anything we don't ask for?"

Granger left the room and came back with new storyboards under his arm. He presented ten of Warren's and my commercials. The client bought three on the spot. All three went on to win many awards and led me to a rather remarkable -- and surprising -- evening at the International Film and TV Festival.

Along with a number of other JWT creatives, I was invited to attend the annual gala -- which required the renting of a tuxedo and putting on one's "company" manners. I was sitting next to Bernie Owett when two of New York's most distinguished copy-writers rose to give the evening's remarks. Shirley Polykoff of Foote Cone & Belding would earn election to the Advertising Hall of Fame for her work on Clairol ("Does She...Or Doesn't She?"). She was joined by Lois Gerachi Ernst, who went on to found Advertising to Women.

> SHIRLEY: "Who wrote the best TV commercials this year? That's our point. Now for the first time (the) International Film and TV Festival presents the UN-COPY CAT AWARD for the outstanding TV advertising copywriter of the year. For originality and persuasiveness in commercial television writing. For both moving words and selling concept and visual idea."

> LOIS: "At last an award to that person on whom all our cameras and actors and sets and action depend -- the writer who had the idea in the first place and made it work. By the way, Shirley -- who wrote those beautiful Kodak commercials this year?"

> SHIRLEY: "Bill Lane of J. Walter Thompson. The UN-COPY CAT of the year."

The applause continued until, duh, I realized I was expected to make an acceptance speech. I can't recall a single word I said but, as I looked out at an audience of my peers, I realized I had been invited to sit at the adult's table.

It's often said that clients get the advertising they deserve. Bad clients get bad advertising, and the good ones – such as Roger Morrison and Bruce Wilson of Kodak – are cause and catalyst for great work. If they had not been there on that day with ears and minds wide open, my ideas would have died leaning against Warren's wall. Roger and Bruce went on to become close colleagues and great friends, with an equal ambition to trail blaze and challenge the conventional wisdom. As an agency, we respected their input and authority. They, in turn, valued JWT's contribution to the success of the Eastman Kodak Company. It was as it should be.

6
A Glass on the Table

"I think you're crazy," Granger said to me one Monday morning in July 1975, not without a sigh. "But if you think you can sell it, go ahead and try." The final Apollo space mission was to launch the next day and I'd been moaning out loud about never having seen a Saturn rocket take off in person. "Write a commercial," Andy Romano said. And so came a modern take on the old advertising yarn about how copywriters create their way to exotic locations:

FADE UP CLOSE ON KITCHEN SINK.
CUT TO WIDE SHOT OF FRENCH RIVIERA.

I sat down at my Royal manual and concocted a small story about a father and son on the beach at Cape Kennedy, filming the next day's launch with their Kodak super-8 movie camera. I figured this simple scenario wouldn't require an expensive director or extensive pre-production. We'd cast people we found right at the scene and shoot it ourselves with other Kodak super-8 movie cameras. The beauty part was a media one. If we succeeded, we would create a storm of positive (and free) PR for Kodak. We'd rush our film to Atlanta to be developed on the spot by the nearest Kodak lab. Then we'd fly it to New York and get it into the hands of editor Howie Weisbrot of Howal Films. We'd record an announcer track that night and lay it back against final picture on Wednesday. JWT senior media people would hand deliver the finished commercial to CBS, walk it through continuity clearance and make sure it aired Thursday night on Walter Cronkite's evening news – while the Apollo 16 was still in space. This was unheard of in the days before portable video cameras and digital imaging.

Roger Morrison and Bruce Wilson of Kodak questioned my sanity, bought the script, and approved a small budget -- all during the same phone call. The great J. Walter Thompson machine then went into action. I kidnapped producer Art Kling and filled him in. "When are we going?" he asked. "Tonight," I said. "Buy a toothbrush." Flights were booked, cars were rented and a fleabag motel somewhere between the Orlando airport and Cape Kennedy was located. VIP passes to the launch area were secured. One final hurdle. We needed some walking-around money and the banks were closed. These were the days before ATMs, so we went to the Meeting Club and passed the hat. A little more than a hundred bucks later, we were on our way.

The episode went pretty much according to plan. The motel might have had a few more fleas than we had counted on, but little matter. We were on the road before first light and our credentials got us as close to the launching pad as could be got. This was a joint mission with the Russians, and there were celebrities from both countries on hand. Although we didn't see him, the Soviets were represented by Ambassador Anatoly Dobrinin. Our side included (how American) John Denver and Shirley Temple. After several nerve-wracking countdown holds, there was sudden thunder under our feet as we filmed the giant Saturn rocket climbing in slow motion towards outer space on Apollo's last flight.

On Thursday evening, a Kodak movie camera commercial, showing the launch of Apollo 16 aired on Walter Cronkite -- while the astronauts were still in orbit. And that's the way it was.

They weren't called the go-go 70s for nothing. Clients dared big and agencies reached far. Research was used to inform rather than restrict. Budgets bloomed and accountability was measured in quality and caché rather than test scores. If you tried large ideas and failed, you were invited to try again. (One commercial I wrote was about the convenience of carrying a Kodak Pocket Instamatic camera while traveling. The spot begins with a long shot of an eagle soaring overhead. Through a series of dissolves, the eagle gets closer and closer until we can see that it's holding a Pocket Instamatic in its talons. Everything was working out fine. We found a trained eagle. His handler taught him to hold the camera. He took off for his big moment – and never came back. A devastated Warren Aldoretta called Roger and Bruce and gave them the bad news. "Go find another eagle," they said, "and shoot the spot again.")

It was in the 70s that the big jingle found its stride, sometimes becoming a hit record (Bill Backer's wonderful "I'd Like to Teach the World to Sing" for Coke comes to mind). The best of the commercial film production companies were experimenting with techniques that kept them ahead of the filmmaking curve. The non-linear, quick-cutting style of many of today's movies and episodic television programs owes much to 70s commercial directors who found inventive ways to tell saga-size stories in small snippets of time.

Nobody lived advertising's 70s any fuller than I did. Invited by my creative director to color outside the lines and encouraged by Kodak to bring them ideas "we haven't asked for," I was also protected by an account team that, when I strayed from true north, found all manner of ways to say: "What Bill really meant …" I was like a kite. The breeze was up and they just kept letting out the string to see how high I could fly.

I didn't fly alone. One day, a new creative partner appeared at my doorstep in the scruffy form of Michael Millsap. He had fierce eyes and a beard that recalled Che Guevara. His mad mop of hair looked that way because he only combed it with his hands. After graduating from Art Center in Los Angeles, Millsap hitched a ride to New York City with, to paraphrase E.B. White, "a portfolio in his suitcase and an ache in his heart." He was hired as an art director, but wanted to produce. Had I let him, he would have written everything, too. His appetite for life was enormous and his drive to create was relentless. As a team, we would become notorious.

Our extended family stretched into account management. Like proverbial cats and dogs, reps and creatives are not inclined to get along. But in Gerry Broderick, Chuck Balestrino and Ernie Emerling, we found intellectual equals, boon companions and a fine offensive line.

Looking as if he had just popped over from Saville Row, management supervisor Gerry Broderick was the first person I ever knew who didn't buy his clothes off the rack. The small cigarette pouches tailored inside the front flaps of his suit jackets facilitated a two-pack-a-day habit. His persuasive way with a client was unequalled. We once almost came to blows after a successful presentation in which I'd played the major part. "Sit down," he told me. "I had that thing sold before you walked into the room." Of course he had, but that didn't keep me from rising up in righteous indignation. Fortunately, we foreswore fisticuffs in favor of martinis. On St. Patrick's Day, Gerry was known to destroy the decorum of the Meeting Club by blaring the Notre Dame fight song on a boombox. And as Fridays rounded midnight, he could be counted on to recite the entire 130 lines of *The Love Song of J. Alfred Prufrock* from memory.

Burly Chuck Balestrino entered the agency business straight out of the Marine Corps and came equipped with only one working gear: forward. He tended to view life and advertising in black and white and was not shy about expressing his opinion in a manner that would frighten small children and their pets. But if he happed to be on your side, you were glad to be in the same foxhole. And, despite all the bluster, he was known to lend you his couch for a month after your wife threw you out of the house.

Ernie Emerling was as tall as a power forward and, fortunately, as gentle as a Quaker. He knew every client political rope, paved every production way, cleaned up after we'd made a mess of things, and once cut off my necktie with a carving knife at a Kodak Christmas party. Good ol' Ernie replaced the tie with an identical one the next week. It wasn't until sometime later in the month, when I was 5,000 miles away in Sao Paulo dressing for a client dinner, that I discovered he had replaced it in a child's size. Good ol' Ernie.

As time went on, the line between our professional and personal lives was blurred, if not erased. The day's advertising passion would typically spill over into the Meeting Club after hours. One or two martinis later, we would often repair to a little French restaurant across the street called Le Cheval Blanc, where René would prepare us one more martini and Madame would hold a table for us should we choose to stay.

More than likely, we would head out to meet girlfriends and wives for dinner. At the first whisper of Kodak, one of them would place a glass in the middle of the table. Anyone who spoke business was obliged to put a quarter in the glass. Inevitably, a word would slip and a quarter would hit the glass. The spell broken, other quarters would plink in rapid succession. One night, Chuck drew a large bill from his wallet and announced that he would talk Kodak as much as he damn well pleased. At meal's end, there was always enough money in the glass to buy flowers on our way to The Grenadier for nightcaps and cabaret. *Have Some Madeira M'Dear*, Richard Shadroi would sing. And so we would.

During the mid-70s, Kodak embarked on the most expensive and daring new-product introduction in its history. There was much cloak and dagger involved, and our first meeting on Product X was held in secret and behind locked doors. There had been whispers about Kodak getting into the instant camera category to challenge long-dominant Polaroid and that day the whispers came true.

Our hearts sank. The "thing" that Kodak engineers pulled out of a bag looked like an old desk telephone – and not a Princess. Polaroid had just unveiled its sexy SX-70 – immediately regarded as a classic example of contemporary American industrial design. We found ourselves looking at a black blob. The true benefit of the Kodak Instant camera, they told us, was that it would deliver pictures of superior quality to any a Polaroid could produce, with true colors never seen before from an instant product.

The task of introducing this albatross fell to Millsap and me. We tried a number of campaign ideas that, for one reason or another, failed to fly. Then, while experimenting with the product one day, a notion hit me. Pictures didn't emerge fully formed from the camera. Their colors came to life gradually. It was as if they were being painted. "Kodak Instant cameras and film," I wrote. "They almost paint your pictures." Aha.

Who better to represent that notion in a Kodak Middle American way than Norman Rockwell? So, we designed a number of commercials, featuring Rockwell, in which the painting he was making was revealed at the end – in a gradually developing Kodak instant picture. Millsap was dispatched to Stockbridge, Massachusetts to meet with the great man himself and show him our storyboards. As Mike tells it, Mrs. Rockwell greeted him at the door, invited him in and said "Norman will be right back. He's out riding his bicycle." When he returned, Rockwell liked the idea just fine. Kodak didn't. "This is about pictures, boys," management said, "not painting."

(If we had studied recent client/agency history more carefully, we would have known better. During the 50s, Kodak sponsored "The Adventures of Ozzie and Harriet," then one of the most popular shows on TV. As part of the deal, Ozzie and Harriet were obliged to appear in Kodak commercials. One such spot featured the Nelsons in the living room of their home – not a set – but their actual residence. As JWT screened the rough cut for the Kodak clients, they interrupted – and erupted – half way through. "What are those paintings doing in our commercial?" they demanded to know. When told that this is how Ozzie and Harriet's living room really looked, Kodak was outraged. They regarded painting as competition for photography and ordered the agency to reshoot the spot – this time with photographs on the walls.)

There was a lot of nervous going on in Rochester. The advertising decision on this product was not going to be left to the advertising people. Top management would weigh in. And they just couldn't wrap their literal minds around the likes of painting and Norman Rockwell. No, this was serious business.

Millsap and I finally succumbed. We gave Kodak exactly what they wanted: a big important campaign (cue the helicopter-shot opening) with big important music (from the Broadway musical *The Wiz*) and a big important announcer (take two, Eli Wallach). Of course, to sell it, we'd have to put on big important presentations, which we did to each level of Kodak management, up to and including CEO Walt Fallon. Fortunately, Mr. Fallon laughed in all the right places and sent us off to shoot what just might have been the most expensive package of commercials developed to that date.

We commandeered the entire town of Mendocino, California and held it hostage for two weeks. With a vow of Omerta, each citizen became part of our secret and a member of the cast. The mayor played a priest, the chief of police a circus clown. Because there was a woeful lack of communications to the outside world, Millsap had AT&T install a long-distance line directly into his room at the Mendocino Hotel, a $10,000 item that is still recalled with awe wherever expense-account tales are told.

Somehow, Howie Weisbrot made sense of it all, transforming thousands of feet of film into sixty-second pieces of poetry. Howie was the third man ever elected to the commercial editor's hall of fame and watching him work was like watching Bernstein conduct the New York Philharmonic. His podium was a Moviola – a marvelous rickety-tickety Rube Goldberg-like contraption that, in 1979, was awarded an Oscar all its own. With a trim basket to the right of him and a film splicer to the left, Howie was a blur of white-gloved hands and pirouettes. As much as any copywriter, art director or producer, Howie was a vital member of our creative team.

It was a daring decade, with an emotional landscape that had its peaks and, ultimately, its valleys. Although we introduced a number of new cameras with great hope and fanfare, these were the very same products that predicted the arc of Kodak's unexpected decline. And, while our tight little group enjoyed considerable professional success, all of us – save Ernie – would be on second marriages by decade's end.

7
A Brand to Believe In

Kodachrome
They Give Us Those Nice Bright Colors
They Give Us the Greens of Summers
Makes You Think All the World's a Sunny Day
I Got a Nikon Camera
I Love to Take a Photograph
So Mama Don't Take My Kodachrome Away©

Other than the light bulb, it's hard to think of a consumer product that touched the lives of everyday people in the 20th Century so profoundly as Kodak film. It makes for a fascinating study in branding and belief. You can neither see Kodak film nor touch it. You can't taste it or smell it. You don't see the results for hours, often days, sometimes weeks. Yet this small miracle of art and science has been loved and trusted by millions, almost without exception.

JWT had a great deal to do with Kodak film's remarkable success. Not long after World War I, the notion of "capturing important moments in your life" was sown and grown. Before then, photo albums were primarily filled with stiff, formal portraits of unsmiling relatives and the occasional coffin shot of the dearly departed.

Instead of comparing product attributes to those of competitors or relying on price cutting to gain market advantage, Kodak film advertising acted as if no other film existed. In creative execution, it tended toward the emotional. That it never tipped over the edge to treacle is a tribute to the restrained touch of, among others, Granger Tripp, Alan Anderson and Ken Thoren.

Within the advertising community, the Kodak film account was among the most prized. And – for the better part of a decade – that prize sat in my office. It was only a year or so after I'd returned from the Army that I was asked to help solve a nettlesome problem. Kodak's absolute dominance in the category was being challenged – just a bit – by a new group of "private label" brands, which sold aggressively against Kodak based solely on price. ("Just as good as – for less!") The challenge was to blunt their thrust without acknowledging their presence or, God forbid, stooping to a price war. I simply turned the price equation around to Kodak's favor by posing a headline question: "Would you trust this moment to anything less than Kodak film?"

This caused a small sensation. Quickly adopted as the theme for all Kodak film advertising, "anything less" was immediately challenged in the courts by the private label manufacturers, who accused Kodak of unfairly representing their film as inferior. Though Kodak lawyers waged a spirited defense for a year or so, the courts eventually ruled in favor of the private labels. Creatively, we were back to square one.

As I sat down to write, I recalled a line I'd use to close a two-minute commercial the previous year – one that died on the vine. "When you want to remember the times of your life," the copy went, "remember Kodak film. And Kodak film will remember you." While that was a clumsy mouthful, I leaned on it as place to begin.

The next words I wrote made me stare at my typewriter for a very long time. No matter how long I looked, it never invited me to write alternatives or, indeed, another word. I walked it down to Granger.

"Let's go see Fred," he said. Fred was Fred Kittel, senior art director of the Tripp/Kittel group. In about a week, we made a creative presentation in Rochester that was notable for its lack of dazzle.

"What pictures are you going to show?" the client asked Fred?

"I don't know. We haven't taken them yet."

"And, Bill, what's the copy going to say?"

"I don't know. I haven't seen the pictures yet."

And so was born "Kodak film. For the Times of Your Life." More readily remembered now as television and song, "Times of Your Life" actually began as a print campaign – one in which Fred and I tried to affect a deep streak of behavior imbedded in most amateur picture takers. In the days before "One Hour Photo" stores, people would send their exposed film to a Kodak lab for processing. On occasion, as a sort of rump research, we'd visit the labs and watch as pictures rolled off the print drums. They pretty much all followed the same pattern. The first couple of pictures were taken around Easter. There'd be a few shots of somebody blowing out birthday candles, several of the family on vacation and one of aunts and uncles gathered around the Thanksgiving turkey. Finally, there'd be a burst of activity on Christmas morning to finish out the roll.

Setting off to convince people that there is much more to life than birthday candles and roast turkey, Fred and I conspired ways to show them the countless other moments that define their lives; and how to use their unique, individual perspectives to provide broader context and lend deeper meaning. Not incidentally, if we could expand their horizons just a little bit and tease them into buying even one additional roll of film a year, you'd need more than ten fingers and ten toes to calculate the increase in profit to Kodak.

Fred engaged photographer Tom McCarthy, whose specialty was shooting on the fly and who had a reputation for putting everyday people at their ease. Because using models wouldn't give us the necessary surprise and spontaneity we were after, we hatched a plan to shoot circles of friends. We'd gain the cooperation of a core one or two family members or old chums, then throw a pebble into their waters, taking advantage of ever expanding situational opportunities. A Sunday school class became a church picnic became a sunset hayride became a fireside ghost story. A high school graduation became a senior prank became an all night party became breakfast on the beach. And so it went. We returned to New York with almost three dozen situations and in excess of two thousand photographs. Only when Fred had culled them down to three or four per situation, which betrayed an emotion or surfaced an irony, did he show them to me. My approach was simple: let the photographs write the copy. I'd settle on one picture from each situation and, whatever it "said" -- I wrote down.

Though the print campaign set a new high standard for this sort of thing and won every conceivable creative award, Kodak was eager to move "Times" into television. That meant music and at least one big Kodak song spot. Over the years, these had become as much a Kodak trademark as the yellow box. Touching stories were set against the words and music of familiar ballads from the Great American Songbook. A teenage daughter in her prom dress at the top of a stair, suddenly a tomboy no more, descended to *The Way You Look Tonight* by Jerome Kern and Dorothy Fields and triggered a lifetime of memories in the eyes of her father. A more recent two-minute commercial – one that caused some stir when it aired – featured a soldier returning from Vietnam to the tune of *Green Green Grass of Home.*

"Let's write our own song, " I said to Roger Morrison at a calculated moment. *"Times of Your Life* makes a great title and, just think, you'd own it. We might get it recorded and you could have a hit." I laid it on thick. At Roger's invitation, I presented five songwriters or songwriting teams we might approach, including Burt Bacharach/Hal David, Marilyn and Alan Bergman, Neil Diamond, John Denver and Roger Nichols/Paul Williams. I recommended Nichols and Williams because they were currently very hot with two Carpenters chart singles: "We've Only Just Begun" and "Rainy Days and Mondays."

Soon after agreeing to do the project, Roger Nichols called me from California to announce that he and Paul had split as a songwriting team. He said that Hal David had agreed to step in, but it would now cost us double. Understandably, Morrison balked at the price.

"Let me take a shot at the lyric" I said. If it works out, it'll save you fifty grand." Every copywriter thinks he can write lyrics. Most cannot. But fifty grand is fifty grand, so Morrison took a deep breath and sent me off to Hollywood as songwriter by default.

When I arrived in California, I checked into the Beverly Hills Hotel and called Roger Nichols to tell him that I was to be his Kodak lyricist. I could hear his jaw drop.

8

Good Morning Yesterday

I had begun flying between New York and L.A. like a commuter takes the train between Westport and Grand Central. I became the unofficial "copywriter in residence" at the Beverly Hills Hotel, which sent a Christmas card one year thanking me for the 104 nights I'd spent with them since January. Called "The Pink Palace" by locals, the hotel more than made up in mojo what it lacked in modernity. The hallways were dark, narrow and wallpapered in dreary palm leaves. The rooms were small, cramped and attractive only if you fancied a color palette of pink and green.

But, oh, the Beverly Hills Hotel had buzz. Things happened there. For decades, Hollywood had cut its deals at breakfast in the Loggia or over cocktails in the Polo Lounge. A and B-listers were always right at "that table over there." You might see members of Richard Nixon's Committee to Re-elect, dining on fresh-squeezed orange juice and croissants, as they got word of the Watergate break-in. Or you might be invited, as I was, to share a glass of champagne with Burt Bacharach and Carole Bayer Sager on their wedding night.

It was fashionable to be paged in the Polo Lounge. Bellboys, dressed in green caps and tunics, would roam through the room shouting in their singsong way: "Call for Mister Niven, call for Mister Niven." (In the 1930s and 40s, there had been a famous advertising campaign featuring a bellboy shouting out the sponsor's name in that same singsong: "Call for Phillip Morris. Call for Phillip Morris." It doesn't take a huge stretch of imagination to picture a couple of advertising men, trying desperately to come up with a new campaign for Phillip Morris, arriving at their bright idea while getting liquored up in the Polo Lounge.)

My hundred days a year notwithstanding, I was reminded in ways large and small that I resided at the lower end of the Beverly Hills Hotel pecking order. Here I was, a twenty-grand-a-year copywriter, driving rented Fords from Hertz, in a valet-parking culture of Rolls-Royces and Bentleys. A particularly humbling moment occurred one night when the hotel was the scene of a Hollywood gala, complete with a broad red carpet that rolled from entrance to curb. It just so happened that, at the very moment the glittering guests were arriving for the festivities, I ordered up my car to drive to a dinner engagement with director Stu Hagmann. "Who's got the orange Mustang II?" the valet called out. Beautiful women, dripping in diamonds, tittered. Thick-bellied moguls in tuxedos scoffed. I tittered and scoffed right along with them, went back into the lobby and called a cab.

Roger Nichols had told me to come over to his house –
"but not before 4:00." I was met at the door by a hulking six-foot-
seven-inch bearded man wearing a scowl. Roger's day usually
began in mid-afternoon and lasted until sunrise the following day.

Gruff he was, but, when he sat down at the piano, he was
magically transformed. His outsized basketball-player's hands betrayed a gentle touch and his foul mood gave way to sweet melody.
(Roger had once played backup center to Lew Alcindor at UCLA.
When Coach John Wooden told him he would have to choose between the piano and basketball, Roger chose the piano.)

He finished playing and turned back to me. "What do you
think?" he asked. I said I liked it very much and could hardly wait
to get to work. I began to uncase my Olivetti portable, assuming
we would sit together at the piano and collaborate. "Here's a
tape," he said, handing me a cassette and showing me the door.
"See you tomorrow." I was not Paul Williams or Hal David, and
for that, I was going to pay.

A daily pattern emerged. I would rise early and sit at the
typewriter. I'd press "play" on my cassette machine, then
"rewind," then "play," then "rewind" – all day long – while typing
out lyrics. I'd take the day's work over to Roger – "not before
4:00" – and he would proceed to trash every word.

This went on day after day. Becoming a maid's curse, I
stopped throwing my wadded up pages of lyrics in the wastebasket
and took to just tossing them around on the floor. And each day,
during the brief window of time when I was at Roger's, the maid
would pick up each crumpled page, vacuum the carpet underneath,
then place the pages carefully back on the floor exactly where

she'd found them.

"How are you doing?" It was Ray Fragasso, executive television producer of the Kodak group, on the phone. He happened to
be in L.A. shooting Pocket Instamatic commercials. When I described how my days were going – or rather not going – he said:
"Let's have dinner. Show me what you've got."

I walked around the room, picked up all the wads of paper
and smoothed them out. Then, I sat down at the Olivetti and fashioned a complete lyric from my favorite parts

Good Morning Yesterday
You Wake Up and Time Has Slipped Away
And Suddenly It's Hard to Find
The Memories You Left Behind
Remember
Do You Remember

The Laughter and the Tears
The Shadows of Misty Yesteryears
The Good Times and the Bad You've Seen
And All the Others in Between
Remember
Do Your Remember
The Times of Your Life

Reach Back for the Joy and the Sorrow
Put Them Away in Your Mind

For Mem'ries Are Time that You Borrow
To Spend When You Get to Tomorrow

Here Comes the Setting Sun
The Seasons Are Passing One by One
So Gather Moments While you May
Collect the Dreams You Dream Today
Remember
Will You Remember
The Times of Your Life©

Ray looked down at the lyric, up at me, back down at the lyric, and up at me again. "Perfect," he said. "Perfect. Tell Roger Nichols to cut the demo. Don't forget, he's working for you."

But Roger had one more trick up his extra-long sleeve. All the time I'd been working on my lyric, he'd had Hal David working on another. After cutting our demo, he cut one with Hal's lyric, too. Then he shipped both directly to Kodak. It was evident at first listen that the second demo had badly missed the mark. There was no mention of the Hal David lyric again.

Paul Anka was not the first to record *Times of Your Life*, nor was he our initial choice to appear in Kodak television commercials. With stars in our eyes and the bravery of burglars, we approached the unapproachable Frank Sinatra. Sinatra had just become grandfather to little Angela and was apparently quite smitten. I wrote a script in which he sings *Times of Your Life* in voiceover, then fi-

47

nally on camera, while dancing with Angela in his arms. In lieu of making a commercial payment to him, we proposed setting up a college trust fund for her. To our surprise, he answered the phone and gave the deal a long week's consideration before passing. It was only then that we turned to Paul, the father of five daughters, with a similar concept.

In the interim, we had produced a campaign of four two-minute *Times of Your Life* radio commercials, stylistically aimed at different audience demographics. Arranged and conducted by Artie Butler, we recorded Barry Manilow, Peggy Lee and The Spinners at Evergreen Studios in the San Fernando Valley. Evergreen was large enough to accommodate a thirty-five piece orchestra and Artie used every bit of that.

A newly minted Barry Manilow arrived at the studio, hoarse and cranky from the whirlwind tour his label had arranged for him to capitalize on *Mandy*, his first big hit. From the start, Barry made it evident that he didn't want to be there. After he had given us a less-than-inspired take, Artie pressed the talkback button. "Almost, Barry. One more from the top."

"Do I have to?" he talked back. "It's only a fucking commercial." But it was our "fucking commercial," and we left that night hoping to never hear of Barry Manilow again. Our prayers were not answered.

On the evening of Peggy Lee's session, there was an extra edge to the room. Peggy was noted for being a first-class diva, and all of us – save Artie – were instructed to speak only if spoken to and to walk on eggshells. Artie had planned to lay down the orchestra tracks before Peggy arrived, then record her vocal to playback.

There was a flurry at the door and in walked Peggy – two hours early. "Artie, darling," Peggy said. Pause. "If you'd wanted somebody to sing to playback, you could have hired Helen Reddy." Artie excused himself, rehearsed the band for half an hour, and Peggy Lee sang live.

We recorded country artist Anne Murray in Nashville and encountered an entirely different music world. The arranger prepared no formal charts, just a few hand-scribbled chord changes. As the session was about to begin, an assistant engineer placed a full bottle of Jack Daniels under the chair of each musician. Perhaps we were just caught up in the spirit of the evening, but the band did seem to play better as the night wore on.

Anka, of course, is the singer most famously associated with *Times of Your Life*. We recorded the television track near his home in Las Vegas, with Johnny Harris arranging and conducting. "Johnny and I are flying to New York later tonight to make the record," Anka said. "Wanna come along?" So, I hitched a ride on Anka's Lear Jet and got a full dose of what its like to be with a star in full entourage. Also on board was tennis champion Jimmy Connors. Jimmy was due to sing backup on a song called Paul had written for him and his then girlfriend Chris Evert. Of course Jimmy couldn't sing, but that was beside the point.

That night, at RCA Studios, *Times of Your Life* became the record I had "promised" Roger Morrison of Kodak. He might have been amused to learn that my main job during the session was to keep Jimmy Connors full of beer so he'd have the courage to sing backup on *There Is Nothing Stronger than Our Love*.

Times and *Nothing Stronger* were two of a dozen songs

Paul had recorded for his next album. To determine which would be released as the first single, United Artists conducted a series of consumer tests in Dallas. Listeners were given devices that allowed them to register their positive or negative emotions as each of the songs was played. One song, as they say, blew the doors off.

And so, *Times of Your Life* was released as the first single in late 1975, stayed in the Top 40 for 12 weeks, rose to #7 on the Billboard Hot 100 chart and, in January of 1966, became Billboard's #1 adult contemporary record. It served as the title song of Anka's album, which went gold during the summer.

We had entered the culture.

9
This Old House

Mighty, mighty television. No medium in the history of advertising has had the ability to deliver messages with such power and emotion. And it was in television that *Times of Your Life* created its biggest impact, taking home the Grand Clio for the best commercial campaign of 1976. "Probably no other project in that year," wrote Michael Rivlin in *Millimeter Magazine*, "brought together on a single campaign such a collection of talented, sharp, clever men who combined years of experience and a keen sense of advertising with the sensibilities of artists and filmmakers."

The key players were directors Stu Hagmann of E.U.E and

Fred Levinson of Fred Levinson & Company, music arranger Artie Butler and agency producer Warren Aldoretta. They couldn't have been more different from one another – either in background or temperament. Levinson made his early mark as a cartoonist with a Borscht Belt sense of humor and had been present at the very creation of the commercial film business in the 50s. Hagmann had flirted with shooting features (*The Strawberry Statement*) and gone on to become the two-time DGA commercial director of the year. He had an angel's smile, a devil's streak and a well-earned reputation for manic devotion to detail. Artie Butler came from the roots of Rock 'n Roll, where he had been a "button pusher" at Bell Sound in New York and wound up engineering half of the Brill Building catalogue. In this era, he was Barbra Streisand's conductor, Barry Manilow's arranger and Frank Sinatra's pal. A wonderfully gifted orchestrator, he wanted nothing more than to become a stand up comedian. Sweet Warren Aldoretta had a poet's sense of picture and pace and somehow managed to keep us crazy people grounded on the fringes of reality.

A dozen story spots were conceived for the campaign and three were approved for initial production. Then popular demand jumped in our way. Paul Anka's recording of *Times of Your Life* was climbing the charts and Kodak asked us to come up with a way to feature him in an introductory commercial. As luck would have it, Paul came complete with a "camera ready" family of wife Anne and five adorable daughters – whose lives were chronicled in albums full of photographic memories.

There was no idea to speak of. We'd look in as Anka was actually recording the song. The sight of his family through the window of the recording booth would trigger a lifetime of his memories as told in pictures. (An extended version of the film still serves as a centerpiece of every Anka live performance.) It wasn't great advertising, but it was timely and true and gave us air cover to go on and do the kind of work that would bring us all a measure of regard.

After Oscar Hammerstein's death, Richard Rodgers wrote the lyric for an additional song to be included in the movie version of *The Sound of Music*. In the coda of *I Must Have Done Something Good* is the line:

> *Nothing Comes from Nothing*
> *Nothing Ever Could*©

Nothing comes from nothing. Many of the plots for the series of Times story spots came directly from my own life experience. The only time I ever saw my mother cry was when we were moving out of a simple tract home (her "first new house") in Bellevue, Washington and moving to a much larger and better house in the San Francisco Bay Area. Was she crying from happiness or sadness? Was she sorry to go or happy to get out of there? She wouldn't tell, she wouldn't say and I kept these unanswered questions inside for years.

They popped out in "This Old House" – the story of an older couple moving out of the home where they have raised their family and spent their salad years. Stu Hagmann added texture and depth. "What 'This Old House' says," he told Millimeter, "is not only that 'there are those moments worth capturing; capture them before they're gone.' (This) is a couple who has reached a turning point. Moving out of the house becomes the emotional crossroads of their life and also the thing that's going to give them the strength to go on, wherever they're going."

Hagmann and cameraman Ed Martin chose to echo the image of blowing curtains from an Andrew Wyeth painting called "Chambered Nautilus" to add deep meaning. "The billowing curtains made the house come alive," Aldoretta said, "suggesting a sense of longing, disturbance, and change in the once comfortable domestic situation."

To arranger Artie Butler's ear, the story of "This Old House" was meant be told in a woman's voice. A Paul Anka track would have sounded curiously out of place. The spot wanted the warm, mature voice of the mother. And so America heard a two-minute Vikki Carr interpretation of *Times of Your Life*.

For Christmas, I drew on another story from my family's past. My father had been raised in the country, where, when he had achieved a certain age (all of 9), his job was to raise and fatten the family turkey for Thanksgiving. At the appointed time, it was also his job to lop off its head. The only (and predictable) problem was that my father became emotionally attached to old Tom and couldn't bring himself to do the final deed. So, with his pal at the other end of a dog's leash, he ran away from home. Alas, this momentary act of boyish rebellion didn't save poor Tom's neck in the end.

Well, cutting a turkey's head off isn't exactly Kodak family fare, so I rewrote the tale as "A Time to Sow," which begins with a father and a small boy planting a tree in their yard. A dozen year's later, it has grown tall enough to become the family Christmas tree and the boy is dispatched to cut it down, which, of course, he can't bring himself to do. The commercial ends with the boy and the family decorating the tree – outside – in a steady snow. Same story. Different turkey.

Director Fred Levinson created a snowy December farm scene out of blistering August landscape. He "shot in cold early morning light." writes Millimeter's Rivlin, "with long lenses against a darkened sky." Again the track was critical and Anka was back – but in decidedly different voice. "We asked Anka to interpret our story," recalls Aldoretta, "to think in terms of the boy's stream-of-consciousness, as though he was talking to us." And talk Anka does through the lines "Good morning yesterday, you wake up and time has slipped away." He doesn't hit full voice until midway through the spot, which gives it a chilling emotional lift.

By every measure, *Times of Your Life* was a tremendous success. Both print and television campaigns took top prizes in the major awards shows. The song had become a standard. And, although Kodak never published sales figures, estimates are that Kodak film held more than 80% share of market. Common sense told us that this was a campaign that would go on a long, long time.

But advertising is rarely about a long, long time. And common sense seldom wins the day.

10

A Hole in the Heart

If Granger Tripp was the heart of the Kodak group, Executive Producer Ray Fragasso was its soul. At once, he was Granger's alter ego, his wingman and his comfort zone. Waving an ever-present cigar, Ray lived large and dreamed big. He never met a new film trend or technological breakthrough he didn't embrace and explore. Throughout his career, he demonstrated a discerning eye for young talent and a natural gift to mentor and lead. He was the first to recognize that art directors Mike Millsap and Warren Aldoretta had the stuff of excellent producers. He plucked David Perry and Jeffrey Mayo out of obscurity and set them on their course to production stardom.

I first got to know Ray well in 1971 -- just after I returned from Vietnam. Granger asked me to write a television spot for Kodak XL movie cameras – advertised as having the capability to make "movies without movie lights." Ray was to produce. While kicking around concepts, he suggested shooting in a museum, where using artificial light of any kind is forbidden. Nobody, he said (always looking for a first) had ever shot a commercial in a museum. We could have readily staged the narrative just up the street at MoMa or The Met. But when I showed him the script, somehow my audacious fingers had typed "Italy" and "Ufizzi."

Much to my surprise, the client bought the concept and Italy right along with it. I was further surprised when I was invited to go along (copywriters seldom did in those days). Ray had selected the gregarious Ben Gradus to direct and off we flew to the Continent on an adventure that included a fortnight of singing our way through long, late, wine-fueled dinners, illegally stowing away in the mail car of a high-speed euro train (and getting caught by the caribinieri), attending an audience with the Pope, and me being thrown in a Florence jail for a few hair-raising hours. Such was life on the road with Ray.

As time went on, Ray found himself mentoring more and producing less and paranoia began to eat into his self-esteem. He feared that the success of his young Turks might be compromising his standing with Granger as the go-to guy for leading-edge production. He took to wearing the most god-awful color and pattern combinations in his shirts, ties and sport coats. Andy Romano finally got up the nerve to ask him why. "I've got to dress hip," he said, "to show you young guys I'm not just some "fuddy duddy." When Andy created a simple spot for Kodak film processing – one, which in a different mood Ray would have assigned to one of his up-and- coming juniors – he decided to produce himself. The scenario involved a couple traversing a desert in a Jeep, taking pictures at scenic points along the way. At a crossing in the middle of nowhere, they come upon a mailbox. The woman removes the exposed film from the camera, places it inside a Kodak Mailer, and puts the mailer in the mailbox as an announcer says something like: "You're never farther away than a mailbox from high-quality Kodak processing."

"We've got to jazz this up," Ray told Andy. "Put in an aerial shot so we can follow the action from above, and zoom in just as the girl puts the mailer in the mailbox." Andy protested, saying that it was unnecessary and would cost too much. But when it came to "jazzing things up," Ray was a force of nature and soon enough there was a helicopter in the budget. Warren Aldoretta was scheduled to scout locations in California, but begged off at the last minute due to a family commitment.

"No problem," said Ray and set off to do the scouting himself. Once again he hired Ben Gradus to direct. Going first class all the way, he secured the services of MacGillivray Freeman, the best aerial production company in the business. (They had become the first superstars of the new IMAX movie format and had recently been nominated for an Academy Award for their astounding cinematography on *Jonathan Livingston Seagull*.)

Jim Freeman himself was at the controls of the helicopter that day. With Ray and Ben on board, he headed for Bishop, a tiny town almost a mile high in desolate Inyo County. I got the call on location in L.A. "There's been a terrible accident," Granger said. The chopper had crashed in the high desert. Ben Gradus had been airlifted to the nearest hospital with a broken back.

Jim Freeman and Ray Fragasso were dead.

From that terrible moment on, Granger – though ever kind and supportive still -- was never quite the same.

11
The Winds of Change

Burt Manning rode into town on a rumor. One day he was a group creative director at JWT/ Chicago, the next he was in New York, sitting in upper management territory. He arrived with a beard and a reputation. "He'll drive you bloody nuts," we were told. If the rumor was true, he had been brought in to become the executive creative director of the New York office.

Manning pretty much stayed out of the way during his first few months, leaving us alone to cope with an increasingly complicated Kodak account. For a company that had grown to leadership because of its sensitivity to consumer wants and needs, Kodak seemed to have gone suddenly tone deaf. This was partly due to the hubris that comes from having ruled the photographic category for a century. But the main cause was a rampant corporate paranoia about the future of film. As Gillette was never about selling razors, but blades, Kodak's real business was not selling cameras, but the stuff that goes inside them. Film – plus the chemicals and paper used to process and print – was their golden egg and Kodak could already see signs that technology was about to run off with the goose.

The economics of manufacturing film has a lot to do with

the cost of silver, film's principal image-capturing ingredient. Silver prices rose dramatically during the age of the Instamatic camera, and, consequently, Kodak suffered at the bottom line.

In response, they developed a new camera system called the Pocket Instamatic – not to provide a slimmer, more convenient camera for the consumer (as advertised), but to cut the size of the negative it produced virtually in half. The quality of the resulting pictures suffered, but profits went up. (In later years, they introduced the Kodak Disc camera, cutting the negative size by half again and -- well, you get the increasingly fuzzy picture.)

The major imaging breakthrough of the 60s was the advent of videotape technology for the general market. Far-sighted companies such as Sony and Panasonic began to develop portable video cameras for consumer use. These would allow people to take non-film "movies" and view them right away on their home televisions.

But, instead of getting into the videotape business (which they could readily have done), Kodak sent their engineers off to invent a super-8 movie camera with sound. "Here Come the Talkies" ads proclaimed to deaf ears. (Full disclosure compels me to admit that I did the ads and commercials – and they were awful.) Even as Kodak was preparing to fight the battle, videotape had already won the war. For the first time in a long time, consumers bought what they wanted, not what Kodak wanted to sell them.

In an even-more dramatic misstep, it was Kodak that invented and patented the original technology that led to the digital camera revolution. But, at least partly because point-and-shoot digital cameras for the consumer market would threaten their film franchise, Kodak sat on the technology, eventually – and, in retrospect, foolishly -- licensing it to foreign competitors.

Kodak's crystal ball was broken. They failed to see the enormous consumer potential in digital photography. Instead, they invested their millions in developing and marketing a product the world neither wanted nor needed: an alternative to Polaroid instant cameras.

All this fumbling around was causing considerable unrest in Rochester. One by one, members of a new management order began to appear. They had not been promoted through the system via engineering, sales or marketing – as was the traditional Kodak practice – but had been born in business school. (A case could be made that the decline and fall of Western Civilization coincides exactly with of the rise of the Almighty MBA.)

Unrest at a client inevitably leads to unrest at the agency. One day, I got a call from Burt Manning – who had indeed become executive creative director of the New York Office – inviting me to dinner. He said it was urgent.

It certainly was expensive. He took me to Le Perigord, then one of Manhattan's toniest restaurants. Burt has never been one for small talk, but he did his best imitation of civil conversation over a drink. After we ordered, he got down to business. "We've decided to make a change," he began. "We want you to take over the Kodak group from Granger."

"I can't do that to Granger," I said.

"We've already decided to make the change. If you won't do it, we'll find someone else who will. Call me in the morning." We didn't chitchat over coffee.

Instead of taking a cab home, I chose instead to walk from 52nd Street and 1st Avenue to my apartment on East 84th, trying as best I could to clear my head. I got in after 11:00, but decided to call Granger anyway. I asked him what he thought about all this. "About all what?" he asked. He didn't know. Nobody had told him.

Manning and New York general manager Ron Sherman had recently declared -- to JWT employees and the world at large -- that "Creative is King." As of this day forward, they said, slumbering J. Walter Thompson was determined to shed its image as a stodgy, account management-driven agency and to raise the level of its advertising product to compete for every award and for every new business prospect who valued creative above all. The playing field had been left to the boutiques long enough. We were out to prove that good big agencies could beat good small agencies at their own game.

I was not carried into my new job on the shoulders of a faithful following. Long-term members of the group were understandably upset about what had happened to Granger and resented having to report to somebody new – especially to the youngest among them. I spent my first days trying to restore calm, to quench hard feelings and to gain consensus. Burt set me straight. "We've put you there for a reason," he told me. "Do what you do. Make the work better."

With that blunt challenge, I changed the temperature of the Kodak group. We began to work hotter, demand more originality, and question every square inch of the status quo. My bedside manner was less grandfatherly than Granger's. I tended to raise my voice. Instead of inviting and nurturing, I pushed and prodded.

We began to play up-tempo and fast break. As a consequence, some of Granger's closest allies chose to move to the sidelines and gave way to an impatient new guard.

Others chose to seek new assignments. Senior Writer Bob Judd and Uber Art Director Sven Mohr had created a wildly popular campaign for the Pocket Instamatic Camera featuring "Little House on the Prairie" star Michael Landon. Understandably. they considered themselves every bit my equal and were not about to start taking creative direction from "that guy Lane."

Though I knew neither of them well, it turns out Sven and I were Gemini twins. We both had started at Thompson as very young men and been singled out in our different regions to attend exclusive JWT training programs -- the Danish Mohr in Noord-wijk, Holland, and I in Delavan, Wisconsin. Achieving much early, we were elected Vice Presidents of the Company on the very same day and, from opposite corners of the world, ended up under the creative leadership of Granger Tripp.

With my promotion, our paths diverged. Sven accepted an opportunity to join Campbell-Ewald -- to help that Detroit-based agency establish a "New York presence." A few years later, feeling a Thompson tug, he came back to the fold, joining JWT/Group sister agency Lord, Geller, Federico & Einstein.

As so many who passed through Thompson, Mohr looks back with pride at the part he played – ever so briefly – in a special time at a special place. "I had indeed been there at the Camelot moment," he said later. "And I had counted for something. I was not Arthur, not Lancelot, but I still sat at the Round Table." Much later in our careers, our stars would cross again.

The diplomacy of Gerry Broderick, Chuck Balestrino and Ernie Emerling eased this cultural transition with the client in Rochester. While Roger Morrison and Bruce Wilson had, in fact, been quietly encouraging the change for some time, the new management order that had been installed above them chose to mess with success.

The concept of "client conflict" had forever contained one of the inviolate taboos in the advertising business. If an agency has a relationship with, say, Coca Cola, it is not -- repeat not -- to have even a hint of a relationship with Pepsi.

But -- who knows when and why -- advertisers determined that polygamy was okay if it applied to their relationships with agencies. And so, while married to J. Walter Thompson, Kodak began to date Young & Rubicam on the instant camera business. "Our account may be getting too big for you," they said. "We may need an extra agency resource." On the face of it, this is a supercilious notion. JWT had long effectively managed much larger accounts than Kodak and could provide "extra agency resources" from any of its 55 offices in 24 countries around the world. Nevertheless, Kodak invited Y&R to present ideas, telling us that we could present ideas, too – if we wished.

Kodak Instant cameras had been a troublesome proposition from the beginning. Because of Polaroid, they filled no real or perceived need in the marketplace. In design and performance, they were me-too to such a degree that they might have been me-three. Their motorized models were decidedly less sexy than the SX-70, and, as if that were not burden enough, Kodak chose to introduce a cheaper model with no motor at all. One literally had to "crank" out the photos. The world dozed.

Manning had long resented the creative independence of the Kodak group and used this episode as an excuse to import two of his favorite people from the Chicago Office to head up our "extra agency resource." Copywriter Tom Hall was a larger-than-life salesman who had the regrettable habit of selling clients concepts he couldn't deliver. His partner, art director Ed George, acted as Tom's designated laugher during presentations, but otherwise was famous for saying absolutely nothing – not to clients, not to colleagues, not to anyone. He wasn't just shy, he was a clam. After about six months of watching this act, client Dick McCoy pulled Chuck Balestrino aside and told him that Kodak would be well pleased never to see Too Tall Hall and the Clam ever again.

That effectively sealed our fate with the Instant camera business and it went off to Y&R to die an inglorious death upon court rulings that Kodak had violated a basketful of Polaroid patents.

It would have ultimately died under the weight of its own stupidity anyway.

12
Too Long at the Fair

On July 13, 1977, at precisely 9:38 p.m., the lights went out in New York City. In a way, it was an omen. At that moment, Warren Aldoretta and I were on the 12th floor of the Graybar building, putting the finishing touches on the Big New Film Campaign we were to present the next day in Rochester before Kodak senior management.

Suddenly, we found ourselves in the clutch of a full-blown blackout, the likes of which had not been seen in the City since 1965. As locals tell it, 1965 was a "good" blackout – the kind where cocktail-party people received points for simply having been there. "Where were you when the lights went out? Oh, dahling, that's so cute. Let me tell you where I was." There was nothing cute about this blackout. Neighborhoods exploded. Couches and television sets walked down the street. Rioters broke through the windows of Brooks Brothers. Those expensive new suits must have looked swell at their arraignments. (Almost 5,000 were arrested that night.)

That there was a request for a Big New Film Campaign at all was odd on the face of it, but predictable in the way these things go. *Times of Your Life* had been successful beyond all measure and should have had legs to run a marathon. But the new MBA class at Kodak, eager to leave its mark, had decided it was "time" for a change, and so we obliged. New clients, as a rule, abandon existing brand campaigns long before they have worn out their welcome with the public. In a Pentagon sort of way, every new administration feels the need to find new enemies. The enemy of the moment was Fuji film from suddenly powerful Japan, which was biting at Kodak's heels and making them damn mad.

So, I went back to the typewriter in search of the truth in eight words or less. I resisted all temptation to enter into an "us vs. them" comparison of emulsion layers, or a fool's discussion about which film produced the greenest greens and the bluest blues. As it turned out, the answer was a pretty simple one at that: For a century everybody's life story in these United States had been told on Kodak film. The evidence was inside every picture frame and filled every photo album. Try as they might, relative newcomer Fuji would never be able to make that statement.

I showed the new theme around and even Manning gave a nod. The rhythm of the words begged for a song, so I called Roger Nichols. Roger had long-since apologized for the whole *Times of Your Life* dust up, and we'd become rather good friends. With just a title to work with, he wrote a beautiful melody. As usual, he made the bridge a challenge, which caused me a bit of hair pulling. But, at the end of it all, Kodak's Roger Morrison and Bruce Wilson thought we might just have ourselves another hit.

Warren and I devised a unique way to introduce the new campaign. It involved Kodak taking sponsorship of an entire hour's program, during which there would be only three commercial breaks – at the program's beginning, midpoint and end. We created a single story to be told in three two-minute segments. For our presentation, Warren produced a sequence of storyboards befitting a movie. Tickets for an early morning flight to Rochester on the 14th were booked. Kodak senior management had cleared their calendars for two hours that afternoon. Everything was loaded into presentation bags and we were on our way out the door.

Then the lights went out. Darkest Africa was never darker than the Graybar Building was on July 13th, 1977. As it was almost 10:00 p.m., Warren and I were the last two creative people still on the floor. Our first task was to find each other. A ghostlike guard, following a thin beam of flashlight, came toward the direction of our calling voices. The three of us sat together awhile, expecting the lights to go back on any minute, as they usually do. Then another guard, who had been listening to a transistor radio, came by to tell us that Con Ed transformers had blown up all over the City and that we were probably in for a long night. The trains and subways were down. Traffic signals were out. Airports were closed.

"We've got to get out of here," I said. "We've got a presentation tomorrow."

"Everybody sit tight," the guard said back. "We're not going anywhere."

Twenty dollars later, Warren and I, presentation bags in hand, were inching down twelve floors of dark stairwell, our backs to the wall to keep our bearings, a guard and his small flashlight leading the way.

Lexington Avenue at 44th Street was in chaos. Because this was the Grand Central area, commuters on their way home had converged by the thousands. Headlights revealed them in an eerie glow. Horns and sirens sounded everywhere. Good citizens, standing in intersections, were trying to direct traffic in vain. Warren, who had no way to get home to New Jersey, planned to stay the night with me up on 84th. As we began our long slog north, we noticed knots of people roaming like gangs. We heard the sound of breaking glass. Street vendors appeared on corners selling flashlight batteries for five bucks apiece.

Once we arrived at my building, we faced a daunting climb to 16B. Angelo the doorman, who would get a hell of a tip this Christmas, led the way up. Finally safe inside, I handed Warren one of the two cold beers from my refrigerator and we took stock.

If the lights came back on during the night, and the airports re-opened in the morning, we'd fly. If not, well surely Kodak would understand.

The phone rang at 6:30 a.m. It was Roger Morrison of Kodak. "You guys are still coming aren't you?"

"Jeezus, Roger. The power's out, traffic's impossible and the airports are still closed."

"Well, you know," he said, "our management is expecting you. What am I supposed to tell them?"

Warren and I decided to head for LaGuardia. As soon as the airport opened, we'd beg or threaten our way onto the first flight to Rochester. We made one final check of our presentation bags to make sure everything was there. Oops. I had left the music sitting on my desk in the Graybar building. Without it, we had no presentation.

I put on my jogging clothes, skipped down the 16 floors of my building, ran to 44th and Lexington, climbed the 12 floors to my office (that took another twenty dollars), fetched the tapes, went back down the 12 floors, ran back to 84th Street and climbed up to 16B.

By some miracle, Warren and I got a cab to LaGuardia. The airport finally opened and we caught a flight that would arrive us only about an hour late for the meeting. "You're going to be late?" Roger said when I called him with the good news. "They won't be happy."

And so, Warren and I, unshaven and smelling like a high school locker room, walked into an ungrateful conference room at about 3:00 on July 14th to present the New Big Film Campaign.

Warren spread out Part I of what we called our "Trinity." The story begins in America and centers on a young man of 18 or 19 years. Through family photographs, he's discovered his roots and become fascinated with the Ireland of his father's father. Through the course of the two minutes, he resolves to visit the old country. Distant relatives still live there and arrangements are made. The new song sets the scene:

Born with the Pride of My Father
I Was Born with a Place to Be From
When I Was Just a Babe
I Had History to Hold Me
In Photographs That Told Me
From Where I Had Come

Bred with the Love of My Mother
I Was Bred to Be All I Could Be
To Carry Inside
The Love and the Pride
That Was Born and Bred In Me

Part II continues in Ireland. The boy meets his new/old family. Bonds are forged and memories are made. He realizes that he is a part of something bigger than himself and in the long line of a great tradition. He makes new friends, one in particular. Bits of conversation, sound effects and an orchestra underscored the picture. ("Notice how Mike Nichols is pre-lapping the sound from the next scene by starting it in the previous one? We may be able to use that.")

> Part II ends with a vocal bridge:
> *I Am Older Than I Am*
> *I Began Before My Time*
> *In the Never Ending Rhythm*
> *Of an Everlasting Rhyme*

In the third part of the story, the boy returns to the United States – but not alone. With him is the girl he met in Ireland. He has brought her home to meet his parents. The song concludes:

> *Born to Belong to a Woman*
> *I Was Born to Be Yours Can't You See*
> *To Love and to Care*
> *To Give and to Share*
> *What Was Born and Bred In Me*©

During the course of the three commercials, there is no spoken announcer copy. At the end of Part III, the screen fades to black and the new theme fades up for the first time: "Born and Bred on Kodak Film."

The dynamic in the room was such that no one was going to speak until we had heard from the head MBA – a rather brusque man named Phil Samper – who apparently had had some unhappy involvement with JWT in Latin America.

"You know," he said finally. "I just don't think we're going to do this kind of advertising any more."

That night, I sat next to Chuck Balestrino on the plane ride back to New York City. As we descended towards LaGuardia, we could see the neighborhoods of Manhattan and Queens lighting up one by one. Civilization had been restored to the City, if not order to my universe.

The next day, I walked into Manning's office and told him it might be a good idea if they found something else for me to do.

Part II

13
Culture Shock

If you were on the creative side of things at JWT, there were two words you hoped never to hear: Ford and Detroit. That's where copywriters and art directors who had fallen out of favor with the agency gods were sentenced to do hard time. Historically, while the Ford account and administrative staff were posted to Detroit, a group currently led by Bert Metter did most of the creative work in the New York office. Those of us in the other creative groups considered the Ford guys esthetically crude and terribly out of step.

So, it was with some unease that I sat with Joe O'Donnell in Burt Manning's office late one 1979 evening. A rising star on the account side, Joe had just been named general manager of the

Detroit Office. He had dreams and Manning had motives. "We're going to move Ford car creative to Detroit," O'Donnell said. "We want you to be creative director." Manning added: "It's the most important creative job we have in the Company right now."

Most important or otherwise, I knew I was being invited to step up to a new level in the Thompson hierarchy. Don Johnston, JWT's CEO, pulled me aside a few days later. "Understand this," he said. "You no longer *work* for J. Walter Thompson, you *are* J. Walter Thompson." Kind words, yes, but closer to the bone, the Company doubled my salary. Combat pay.

Nothing quite prepares you for injection into the Detroit automotive advertising world. In 1979, it was a closed society – a Tong -- where initiation was rigorous and acceptance arbitrary. Big Three auto tycoons managed by edict and passed their cocktail of intimidation down through the ranks. Every junior executive at Ford was Lee Iacocca in his own mirror.

These men – and to a one, they were all men – were woefully out of touch with the consumer market. They never had to scrape up the dough to buy a car. Brand new ones were provided to them every three months or so. They never had to suffer long lines at the pump during an oil embargo or deal with a steep spike in gas prices. Their cars were gassed, serviced and washed every morning when they drove into the parking lot under headquarters. (If they went out to lunch, the cars were gassed, serviced and washed a second time when they returned in the afternoon.)

The significant reverses suffered by the U.S. auto industry in the 70s should have delivered a sobering wake-up call. A crippling United Auto Workers strike at the beginning of the decade caused a sharp reduction in U.S. auto production, a void that was readily filled by newly competitive and fuel efficient imports from Japan. The Arab oil embargo of 1973 served to stoke consumer demand for the smaller, gas-sipping Japanese cars even more.

Still the Big Three bullied on, believing they could maintain their preeminence in the world of automobiles by simply imposing their will. Each continued to market lines of almost identical cars through their multiple divisions, hiding them under different skins and nameplates. The Chevrolet Impala was, at the same time, an Olds 98, which shared everything but a badge and a grille with a Buick Regal. A Ford Mustang was a Mercury Cougar. A Dodge Dart was a Plymouth Fury. None, unfortunately, was a Toyota Camry.

It was a shame. For generations, Detroit had stood as the epitome of American ingenuity and influence. Some considered Ford's River Rouge Plant one of the Seven Wonders of the Industrial World. Every bit of a mile long, the Rouge Plant could gobble up massive amounts of steel, glass and plastic at one end and spit out brand new cars at the other – one every single minute. The American car changed how teenagers courted, defined every man's driveway and spread families out all over creation. Without the American car, there never would have been a Route 66, a drive-through window at McDonald's or the chase scene in *Bullitt*. An American car represented dreams, lust and destiny all wrapped up in four thousand pounds of curb weight.

In the shadow of such power and promise, a rather remarkable Detroit advertising community arose and flourished. The local outposts of McCann-Erickson, BBDO, D'Arcy and Young &

Rubicam thrived in a high-octane world all their own, much farther away from New York in state-of-mind than in air miles. When shooting print ads, they turned almost exclusively to a small circle of Detroit photographers who had mastered the art and science of making beautiful images from hunks of reflective steel, chrome and glass. In car circles, an event spoken of in the same breathless tones as the breaking of the sound barrier occurred in 1949. That's when photographer Jimmy Northmore erected a large tent inside the old Detroit Music Hall and discovered how to achieve "white chrome" in the camera. As for television, well not just anybody could shoot car. A handful of Detroit-centric commercial directors dominated the business.

Key agency art directors rarely had to buy their own lunches. With generous print and catalogue budgets at their disposal, they were persistently and passionately courted by reps from the major studios around town. If you wished to take a group photo of the Detroit art director elite, you need only stop by the London Chop House or the Ponchetrain Wine Cellars on any given Wednesday, and you stood a good chance of finding them there – the whole lot. Art directors learned to attend studio Christmas parties in cars with empty trunks. Parting gifts tended to be the size of television sets or home stereo systems.

Creative people in Detroit had fierce pride. They resented outsiders – especially those from New York – who came to town and tried to "big time" them. They might not have been as famous as their New York counterparts, but they had gasoline in their blood and this is where they chose to make their mark.

The poet laureate of Detroit copywriters was Jim Hartzell,

who became forever famous for writing "Baseball, Hot Dogs, Apple Pie & Chevrolet." At Campbell Ewald, he teamed with creative director Jim Bernardin and executive producer Dennis Plansker to prove that game-changing car creative work could generate from a Detroit-based agency. Jack Frakes ran the much-admired Buick group at McCann-Erickson, which spawned a pied piper of a man named Dick Johnson. Johnson jumped to BBDO on Dodge and set out to attract all the young talent in town, forming what he referred to as the "New York Yankees of Detroit Advertising." In 1979, J. Walter Thompson was the only major car agency that persisted in keeping its major creative force in New York. While the Detroit Office maintained a small copy and art director group to handle the odd assignment and service the Ford Dealers Association, the big creative guns fired from a thousand miles away. Even when they came to Detroit for meetings, they occupied their very own suite of offices called "The Caddy Shack" – not at JWT – but at Ford. They were an island apart.

It was into the teeth of this tradition that I landed, charged by Joe O'Donnell and Burt Manning with "establishing a creative presence." I was soon to learn that, not only did I have to buck up JWT's reputation around Detroit, I was going to have to fight a rear-guard action against the existing New York Ford creatives. Evidently, they were not in on Manning's master plan – at least the one he had communicated to me – and had no intention of letting some punks out in the boondocks steal their business.

We had met the enemy, and they were us.

14

Little House on the Prairie

JWT occupied a small three-story building on the open plains of Dearborn. (Careful, now -- that's DEER-bern, not DEER-BORN.) Looming in the distance was the mighty Glass House of Ford World Headquarters. It was as if they were keeping a watchful eye on us.

Joe O'Donnell had made a magnetic first impression on both Ford and the office staff. Often described as "Kennedy-esque," Joe was blessed with an ex-football player's locker-room charm and a 3 handicap. He was also a fine advertising man with a keen sense of a good idea. Most importantly, he had a backbone.

He needed all that to cope with a recently discovered anomaly in JWT's books, laying bare a double-billing error in the seven figures. While the accounting skullduggery didn't happen on his watch, O'Donnell walked point for the Thompson Company, made sure the house was cleaned of offending parties, and proceeded to steer a straight course. "Essentially," O'Donnell says, "we stole a million dollars from Ford, gave it back and kept the account." Joe had earned his chips.

The creative department occupied the 2nd floor of this Little House on the Prairie and was split into two distinct groups. By far, the largest and most able of the groups was General Accounts, which served all non-Ford business, including Champion Spark Plugs and Monroe Shock Absorbers. It was kept completely separate from Ford in order to reassure non-car clients, who forever fretted that the latest Ford crisis would drain them of their dedicated creative resources. General Accounts won its share of awards and, in general, had a pretty good time of it.

A nascent Ford group had been slapped together by Vic Kenyon, an old-line car guy on loan from New York. With nothing else to offer, Vic threw money and titles around like wiffle balls. Senior among his hires was John Gahaghan, whose nose suggested a strawberry and whose manner tended toward the very, very nervous. His business card identified him as an associate creative director. (Rare among Detroit creatives, John didn't drink. It was said that he gave up the sauce after he consumed thirteen Bloody Marys during one lunchtime and disappeared into an alcoholic coma.)

Writer Dick Howting had bounced from BBDO in Detroit to Leo Burnett in Chicago, but bounced back again when "I got tired of writing talking toaster commercials." JWT took him in and called him a group head. There was Burt Markland, who had recently joined from Campbell Ewald. (Burt had once assisted the great Helmut Krone, the most famous of all the groundbreaking Doyle Dane art directors.) Evidently, he was a group head, too. Young Mike Priebe, who had just been rescued from the art bullpen, showed promise. Randy Albright and Ron Deller, a team that simply occupied space and kept to themselves, did not. (The rotund Deller at least provided comic relief. One morning, as he and Priebe shared a ride to the office, Deller experienced a sudden bout of indigestion. Displaying a fat man's logic, he zipped into Donutsville U.S.A. to buy Tums. Of course, they had none. "Okay," Deller said without hesitation, "gimme a donut.")

Two doors down from me sat Bob Colarossi, called "Raisin" for reasons I'd rather not go into, or simply "The Doc". He was wise to the ways of Detroit advertising and, during the coming days, would guide me through treacherous waters. Basically, if you were okay with the Doc, you were okay with everyone in the city.

The office was in a flurry when I arrived. The Detroit group had been given the assignment of coming up with a new commercial for the plain-Jane Ford Fairmont. Time after time, I'd watch them leave for the Renaissance Center, Ford's downtown marketing location, with a presentation bag full of commercials. Time after time, I'd watch them return without having made a sale. Joe O'Donnell advised me to stay out of this one. "Not a good way to make your first client impression." So, I busied myself with settling in. I hired a secretary – the wonderful and unflappable Linda LaPrise – and began familiarizing myself with the reams of information about Ford products and marketing plans. During the coming fortnight, I was put on a steep learning curve by my old friend Chuck Balestrino, who had preceded me to Detroit by about six months. I could swear he looked five years older.

After about a week of sitting back and watching, I called a meeting among the creatives to discuss how we were going to work. First, since it was apparent that none of them had groups, I announced there would be no such title as "group head." We would each be called by what we actually did: copywriter, art director or producer. No senior or junior. No associate this or executive that. There would be no layers. Everyone would report directly to me.

Looking at the work, I quickly discovered who could play and who could not. Howting and Markland were by far the brightest, even though they made a curious pair. One day, Burt rolled Dick into my office in a wheelchair. It seems that, after a recent bibulous evening, Dick had tried to sneak into his apartment the back way. This involved scaling a low wall in the dark that, unfortunately, had a longer drop on the far side than Dick had calculated. He broke both his heels.

As for the rest, well, we needed help. I considered calling for reinforcements from New York, but reckoned – correctly as it turned out – that bringing in people from the outside would fuel resentment. So I turned to Bob Colarossi for his knowledge and wisdom. Bob knew virtually every creative person in town; who was unapproachable; who just might be available at the right price. We wanted only those who were passionate about the work, who were tough enough to fight for their ideas, and who were not concerned with ceremonial titles. Our first hires, I said, should create a buzz that would attract others. Bob, between puffs of an ever-present Silva Thin, discreetly put the word out.

When it comes to its creative community, Detroit is a very small town. Rumors are legal tender and secrets are an endangered species. So, to be on the safe side, Jerry Apoian and Dan Hughes, a team from Young & Rubicam, agreed to meet me at a bar tucked in the back of the Washer & Dryer, a matching set of nondescript buildings across the road from the Little House. Jerry was a writer, but, more importantly, he was one of the most powerful car television producers in the business. Dan had been one of Dick Johnson's New York Yankees. He brought a bright, contemporary eye for the printed page as well as an outsized personality. At first, they were skeptical.

"No titles?" Apoian said.

"No titles," I said.

"No layers?"

"No layers."

With a handshake and a handsome bit of financial bait, we landed our two first significant creative hires and the word flashed around the city. In short order, we added Larry Carroll, a producer/art director with an infectious spirit and paired him with Rik Gloff – a copywriter with an attitude – from Campbell Ewald. Writer Jim Thomas and art director Bill "Dish Face" Morden were not far behind.

Howting. Markland. Apoian. Hughes. Carroll. Gloff. Thomas. Morden. Colarossi. Priebe. We were ready to go to work. Or to war.

The plan had been to shift creative assignments from New York to Detroit as soon as we added people enough to handle them. Now, even as we had our core group in place, New York refused to let go of the hotter car lines and instead handed us only one or two of the troubled ones. None was more troubled than Pinto. As an engineering short cut, Ford had designed the Pinto's gas tank in such a way that it would explode in even a modest fender bender. Instead of fixing the problem, the client asked JWT to solve it with an advertising campaign. Thus was born "The Pinto Family." An enterprising copywriter had discovered that there were a remarkable number of multi-Pinto families strewn across Middle America. If it was so unsafe, the reasoning went, why would a father buy a Pinto for his college-age daughter? This was all well and good, but it seemed that every time we sold a new Pinto Family spot to the client, there would be a fender bender in Cedar Rapids and somebody's college-age daughter would be blown up.

While New York had washed its hands of the bloody Pinto, they continued to do all the dirty work on Ford's most successful car lines. They pretty much pretended we didn't even exist.

As much as I kicked and screamed, my leverage was limited. I still hadn't earned my chips.

15
Ablondi's Belt

It was a moment of considerable confusion. "John Gahaghan thinks he's having a heart attack," Howting said. Gahaghan had gone to the client earlier in the morning to present new LTD commercials. I arrived just as Ford's raging advertising director was rushing out of the conference room and a band of EMTs was rushing in – oxygen tanks, stretchers and all. We watched in horror as Gahaghan was gurneyed to a waiting ambulance.

Later we learned that he hadn't had a heart attack at all -- merely an attack of Ray Ablondi. (Alas, but maybe not, it would be the last we ever saw of Johnny G in a Ford creative meeting.)

If ever there was a more diabolical client than Ray Ablondi, the story has yet to be written. Ablondi combined ignorance, arrogance, bombast and malaprop in a breathtaking display of corporate dysfunction. He was an educated man, having attended the London School of Economics. (But, then again, so had Mick Jagger.) He was a fashionable man, who had an odd quirk: his belt always matched the fabric of whichever expensively-tailored suit he was wearing. The sight of Ablondi's belt was enough to scare brave men into the next room.

It was no wonder that I found fear walking the halls as I arrived in the Detroit Office. The little creative group then in place was so cowed by Ablondi that I invited them to stay back at the Little House if they wished, and to let me suffer the daily slings and arrows at the Ren Cen. Not that I was treated with kid gloves. During my first presentation to Ray, Howting and I lined up a series of ads along a rail on the opposite side of the table from where he sat. He huffed and puffed, boiled and bubbled, then made for the door. In a Colombo moment, he paused just before leaving, turned, and yelled at me to "Get that shit off the wall before anybody sees it!"

Matters came to a head one day just after I had made a spirited presentation of a new LTD commercial. Ray asked me to pass the storyboard across the table. He studied it for a minute, stood up and threw the storyboard back at me on a perfect horizontal. If I hadn't ducked, it would have decapitated me. "This ain't Kodak is it, buddy boy?" he said.

As he rushed out of the room, Joe O'Donnell followed close on his heels. And when Ray went into his office, O'Donnell closed the door behind them. "If you ever do anything like that to my people again," Joe fumed, "I'll have your job."

They say that the rigors of war beget bands of brothers. And brothers we became in the new Ford creative group. It's difficult to imagine a more unlikely collection of marvelous misfits. Writer/producer Jerry Apoian was known as "Beef," at least partly because he managed to stuff a rather oversized body into rather undersized pants. He had a shock of red curly hair and an equally red curly beard. If you'd turned his head upside down, he would have looked pretty much the same. The Beef was our Atlas. He could shoulder an enormous production burden without bending under the pressure. His bible was the Official Airline Guide, which he had memorized right down to the last flight to Fargo. He was out of town on shoots so much that, on more than one occasion, we had to assure the Detroit Metro Airport that he really was coming back to claim his Pontiac Firebird – the one with the frequently flat left rear tire.

In addition to being a talented art director, Dan Hughes happened to be a very good cook. His daily habit was to rise at 4:00 a.m., put a batch of cookies in the oven, go out and wash his car (in the winter, he washed it inside his garage), and be in the office before 6:00 -- bearing fresh cookies and good cheer. An awfully happy man seemed Dan Hughes.

The first time I saw Dick Howting in an internal creative meeting, he was wearing a tall, cardboard mitre, fashioned after the ceremonial headgear of the Roman Catholic Church. As Richard "Cardinal" Howting, he routinely opened such meetings by blessing the work. In physical appearance, he was nothing more than a stick figure hiding behind a cigarette, coke bottle glasses and a bushy moustache. He walked as if constructed out of so many nuts and bolts.

But, oh, how Dick could write. He won my eternal admiration during the initial Fairmont brouhaha. To mask their product deficiencies, Detroit automakers and their complicit agencies had invented a new genre of advertising best described as "cherry picking." If you couldn't come right out and claim with a straight face that your car was better as a whole car (which, the last time we looked is what people actually drive), you simply cherry picked features from different cars to create a positive message. "More head room than a Honda Accord, more leg room than a Volkswagen Beetle and more trunk room than a Chevy Cavalier." All this, alas, usually added up to a car nobody wanted.

"Well, let's give the clients exactly what they asked for," Howting said. "That'll teach 'em." So he wrote a spot called "Mannequins." To demonstrate legroom, he loaded a bunch of disjointed mannequin legs into the front seat of the poor old Fairmont. To show head room, he filled the back seat with a hundred mannequin heads. In the trunk, well, he put mannequin torsos. Upon presentation, Ablondi was speechless. But "Mannequins" was produced and aired to great acclaim.

Howting's partner, Bert Markland, was known as "the world's meanest art director." That was curious; he seemed nice enough to me. Then one morning, I walked by his office just as Dan was bidding him "ay-yo, ay-yo" in that merry way of his. "Go fuck yourself," Bert replied without looking up. Good morning, Bert. In time, we would pair Markland with Jim Thomas, who was known, conveniently, as "the world's meanest copywriter." His explosions seemed to come out of nowhere. One day, Jim was passing kindly secretary Donath Barr in the hallway.

"Howya doin', pal?" Jim asked.

"I don't like to be called 'pal,'" said Donath quietly.

"Okay. Howya doin', asshole?"

Larry Carroll and Rik Gloff considered themselves our macho team. The more they tried to live up to their self-given reputation, the more unintentionally laughable they became. Their saving grace was that they flat out didn't care what anybody else thought. Over time, they wrote and produced their bombastic way to some memorable Mustang advertising.

Every few days – usually near my office – a cartoon would appear, affixed to a doorjamb or pinned to a presentation wall. The caricatures and captions were the product of the rapier-sharp pen of Mike Priebe. With a few quick strokes, he could capture the craziness going on in our mad, mad, mad, mad world and wickedly etch each of our places in it. Not knowing any better, I had selected a white Ford Mustang as my company car. Forever after, I was portrayed driving a Norge washing machine down the John Lodge Freeway. I made the mistake of balancing a storyboard on my head during a particularly long and tedious meeting. Two days later, I was a cartoon. Howting could be shown showering or with a lampshade on his head, but he always held a martini glass upright ("Didn't spill a drop.") Markland's spectacles were always drawn hyper big, which made him look an awful lot like Mr. Magoo. And so it went. One particularly funny panel celebrated Dan's penchant for arriving at the office before dawn in contrast to his partner Apoian's habit of working late. It shows them passing in the hallway. "Mornin', Dan," says an extremely drowsy Jerry. "Night, Jer," says a highly caffeinated Hughes." If there was a director of sanity in the Ford group, it was Mike Priebe.

Among the more important meetings in our endless days occurred during the lunch "hour." As a rule, the presiding officer was the good doctor, Bob Colarossi, who, in fact, never ate. ("Oh, no thanks," he'd say to the approaching waitress. "I've already eaten. I'm just joining my well-hung friends for a drink.") The venue might be pizza at Gracie C's or a fine meal at the Wine Cellars – but it always involved liquor. While most all of us would stop by for a time, Doc was there for the duration. Even on his way out the door, there'd be a healthy shot of Grand Marnier ("The Big O") in his coffee.

Doc was old school when it came to creating layouts and storyboards. He figured there were only so many car colors and so many car angles, and roads all looked the same. So he designed a generic car, drew it from every angle, and created it in every color. He never threw a frame away, but carefully peeled it off its backing and stored it away for later use. When he'd get a new commercial to draw, he'd simply reach into a certain desk drawer for frames showing a red car or into another drawer for frames of a blue one. "Listen to daddy," he said to me, quoting Bill Morden. "Never draw what you can trace. Never trace what you can stat. Never stat what you can steal."

The remarkable camaraderie among these outlaws and ingrates continued over time. Years later – long after the Detroit episode had ended and we were strewn to the outlands – poor,

86

naïve Dan sent a video to us all at Christmastime. It was a warm, good-hearted piece staged in the atrium of an office building. Isolated and indifferent people are sitting around having lunch when a young man walks into their midst and begins playing "Deck the Halls." on the saxophone. A moment later, a young woman with a bell-clear soprano walks up to him and begins to sing. One by one, and then in clumps, others join and there is joyful hullabaloo by the end. Since the Little House had a similar-looking atrium, Dan wondered if that reminded us of our circumstance. "Oh yeah, that was us," Rik Gloff fired back. "Uh huh. Sure. Back in '83. Of course this was filmed AFTER the Christmas Party the night before, which featured the Annual Yuletide Traditions of Snow Bank Crash Test, Parking Lot Urination Competition (three categories: range, accuracy and duration - the Ladies Division was added later.) Sacrifice of the Virgins (now discontinued) and of course the Annual Yuletide Ball Walk. This particular footage brings back special memories. It was shot the next day just before the inaugural Robert C. Colarossi "Hey, Christmas boy, I'm gonna shove that saxophone right up your ass." closing ceremonies - sponsored by Bayer Aspirin."

The account management team resided one floor up from creative and a million miles away. With the notable exceptions of O'Donnell and Balestrino -- who were such allies and champions that we counted them as ex-officio members of the creative group -- the rest were mostly annoying. Occasionally, they could be downright dangerous. An episode with management supervisor Dennis Sinclair – who daily demonstrated why we referred to him as "The Mayor of Dense City" – will serve as a case in point. At the last minute, the client had killed a scheduled LTD shoot and sent us back to the drawing board to come up with entirely new creative. Sinclair walked into my office that afternoon and asked if we were going to show the client a rough cut according to his schedule, which, as I recall, he was waving in the air. "Dennis," I said, "we don't even have a commercial to shoot."

"But it says right here," Dennis persisted, "that we're supposed to show them a rough cut a week from Friday."

"Let me get this straight, Dennis. You want us to show the client a rough cut before we shoot the commercial."

"That's what it says."

That might have been the first time we banned all account people from the second floor. It wouldn't be the last.

16
Getting Nowhere Fast

There must be a special place in marketing hell for the likes of Lee Iacocca. While he was justifiably lionized in the 60s as the "Father of the Mustang," critics conveniently forget that he was also the "Father of the Pinto," Ford's infamous exploding car. He punched his ticket to infamy in the late 70s, when he hooked Detroit and the entire car-buying country on the addictive dope of rebates. As chairman of the Chrysler Corporation, Iacocca wrapped himself in the flag with jingoistic "buy American" commercials, which pandered to the public's basest anti-Japanese sensibilities.

He took us all down with him. Branding and positioning took a back seat to bells and whistles as both Ford and General Motors were forced to follow Chrysler's course along rebate road. Creativity was reduced to the lowest common denominator. Every two months or so, we'd be obliged to invent a newer, better rebate program to "celebrate" something. Since it would have been bad form to admit that our products were in distress, we were always compelled to conjure up some false-whisker event. "Ford's Mileage Leadership Celebration is underway!" The poor, baffled customer. Over time, rebate commercials tended to all swim together in one mindless mess. Networks were awash in giant "cash back" graphics superimposed over cars making "S" turns on mountain roads, zipping along to generic "high-energy" music.

At least, the Chrysler commercials had Iacocca. We countered with Ed McMahon, Johnny Carson's sidekick on *The Tonight Show*. Thinking back now, it isn't clear why we took to wardrobing Ed as if he were the eccentric uncle who visits once a year. "Get out that red vest," Howting would shout from down the hall. The vest in question had become trademark attire for Ed from rebate to rebate and took up residence on the back of my door between shoots. So, on many a Friday afternoon (rebate crushes always seemed to happen on Friday afternoons), I would don the vest and gather the group for what surely would be a weekend's work.

When Ed had worn out his welcome, we replaced him with Telly Savalas, star of television's Kojak. This gave our spots a tough-guy, straight-talk quality that played well in Middle America. Productions with Telly were an adventure in alcohol. Shot at a moment's notice and on a tight schedule, the TV commercials would be filmed during one long day at a Ford dealership in the San Fernando Valley. Jerry Apoian would then put Telly in a limousine and send him off to join me at a recording studio for voiceovers. Problem was, Telly would consume a full bottle of cognac between the set and the studio and, by the time he reached me, getting him to string six coherent words together took some doing. He'd make light of the many awkward moments. "Who loves ya, baby?"

As for doing actual brand advertising, we were caught in a communications twilight zone, a period that lasted into the early 80s. Coming down Ford's design pipeline were so-called "world cars" – forward-looking vehicles that represented a true modern global vision for the company. But, it would take years to get these cars to market and, in the meantime, we had to move thousands of the current models every week. "There's a world of better ideas coming from Ford," we said. Unfortunately, the current ideas were years behind the times.

Symbolic of this was the odd selection of unique car colors one could get from Ford. There was something called "Honolulu Blue," found only on Thunderbirds, the Detroit Lions and leisure suits. There was a pastel yellow and a brown that resembled chicken soup. It didn't help that Ford's head of North American operations and its division general manager – the very two people responsible for such choices – were legally colorblind.

As consumer preference was clearly shifting to smaller cars, Ford chose to introduce a new model of the full-size LTD. Guzzling gas all the way, the anachronistic Crown Victoria was known around our parts as the "Big Vicky." Ford's ills were compounded by the surge in demand for front-wheel-drive technology. The imports had it. Chrysler had it. Buyers wanted it. Yet every car in the Ford garage was defiantly driven by the rear wheels. (Chrysler made quite a splash with its entry into the front-wheel-drive arena with the introduction of its K-Cars. These tin cans were boxy, homely and laughably ill made. But they were cheap and had FWD – perfect for a certain gullible group of buyers, dismissively referred to by Chrysler management as "PODS" – Poor Old Dumb Shits.)

In times such as these, car companies typically turn to cosmetic solutions. The Ford Fairmont was a perfect example. Fairmont was never much more than a basic A to B car that sold at an affordable price. Ignoring the Fairmont's no-frills personality, Ford created a new model with extra chrome and stripes, upped the price, and called it Futura. Its key selling virtue was to be style. As Dan Hughes and I struggled with a creative solution, it became evident that making a compelling case for the Futura on the car's merits alone bordered on the impossible. We needed to borrow interest. So we went in search of an appropriate celebrity who might lend the Futura the style it definitely lacked. At our request, JWT's entertainment group arranged a meeting between me and Lauren Bacall. The elegant Bacall was very much in the news at the moment as author of a best-selling memoir about her life with Humphrey Bogart. We met at her apartment in the Dakota, a hulking, gothic building on New York's Upper West Side. The Dakota had taken on a certain recent notoriety as the scene of John Lennon's murder. Security was understandably tight as I was ushered to Ms. Bacall's chambers. I was greeted by her manager, Tex Beha, a woman more than six feet tall, wearing cowboy boots and a Stetson. In time, Ms. Bacall joined us and I took her through the scripts and storyboards. I remarked to others later on just how gracious she had been. We were to find out on the shoot that the world was populated by two very different Betty Bacalls.

The final client presentation had its moments. Our plot had Ms. Bacall arriving from abroad, to be met at the airport by transportation befitting her celebrity: a Ford Fairmont Futura. Dan Hughes pointed out that the whole scene was to be very upscale, with Betty sporting Louis Vuitton luggage.

"Who in the hell is this Looie Veetin?" Ablondi spat. The more Dan explained, the deeper the ditch he dug for himself. "And what's with the black skycap?" Ray went on, digging his own ditch. "We can't be showing stereotypes." Despite our appeals for truth and reality, our final cut featured the only white skycap in America.

About once every five years, Los Angeles chooses a January to wash into the sea. That was our circumstance as we landed in a monsoon to begin pre-production on the Futura campaign. Stu Hagmann, who has a winning way with star talent, was booked to direct. Though there are few human beings Stu can't get along with, Lauren Bacall turned out to be one of them. On eve of the shoot, we held our final pre-production meeting in Bacall's suite at the Beverly Hills Hotel. We showed up at the appointed time with a group of a dozen or so, including wardrobe, makeup and script people. Ms. Bacall kept us waiting for the better part of an hour and, upon entering, scanned the assembled group. "Young man," she said finally, turning to a figure standing near the door. "Would you please take off that dreadful raincoat?"

"Ms. Bacall," I said. "I'd like to introduce you to Stu Hagmann, the director. "And you," she said, turning to Dan Hughes. "Would you please wipe that smile off your face? You're driving me crazy." And so it went. During the course of the meeting, she managed to offend practically everybody, especially the poor wardrobe stylist, who went running from the room in tears.

I returned late that night from dinner to find one of the Beverly Hills Hotel's distinctive pink message notes under my door. "Please call Ms. Bacall," it said. By default, I had become her go-to guy for all things diva. I dialed her extension despite the hour. "Hello," answered an extremely deep voice.

"May I speak with Ms. Bacall?" There was an agonizingly long pause.

"This *is* Ms. Bacall," the deep voice replied. "Make sure I have cigarettes in the morning," she said. "I can't be without cigarettes." She coughed and hung up.

The shoot was predictably fraught. The weather created havoc, and whatever trouble the storm failed to cause, Bacall provided. Getting her out of her trailer for a shot -- once it had been meticulously and, considering the elements, miraculously lit -- required major coaxing. Every on-camera line proved a dramatic trauma. The word "shit" was said often. Everyone involved tried to forget the entire mess as soon as America certainly did.

There was a bright moment during all of this, one that gave a hint as to where we wanted to take the brand. It began as a notion from editor Howie Weisbrot and was scripted beautifully by

Dick Howting. Ford had just come out with a 25th anniversary edition of the Thunderbird and was looking for a special way to celebrate. Howie's idea was to cut a visual duet between the original 1955 Thunderbird and the 1980 model against a musical duet between Nat King Cole and his daughter Natalie -- two generations of a famous nameplate serenaded by two generations of pop royalty.

"Unforgettable" was unforgettable. After we signed a deal with Capitol Records for use of the original Nat Cole track and with Natalie Cole to overdub her part, I flew west to produce the recording session at Evergreen Studios in L.A. At a crucial moment in the spot – just before Natalie's vocal entrance -- arranger Artie Butler wrote a dramatic segue from the old, rather pinched, track to a contemporary, freshly-recorded one. To fill out the modern orchestra, Artie hired musicians from Nat Cole's last road band. It was an emotional moment when Natalie came into the studio and saw so many old friends. Just before she entered the vocal booth, Artie asked her if she needed a moment to cry.

"No, Artie," she said. "I did my crying a long time ago."

The commercial created such a sensation that Natalie recorded a long version for her next album. This new "Unforgettable" – born from the hearts and brains of Howie Weisbrot and Dick Howting – won the 1987 Grammy for "Record of the Year." Going on the interview circuit to promote the record (including an appearance on *The Tonight Show*), she never once mentioned where the original idea had come from or how J. Walter Thompson had brought it to life.

For the most part, we spent our days suspended in creative limbo. In addition to the troglodyte Ablondi, we had to deal with his chief lieutenant, Bob "The Bobber" Gillooley – a man who deserves a mug shot all his own. Gillooley considered himself a connoisseur of consumer taste and a keen observer of contemporary trends. In actuality, he was a small-minded, slow-witted dilettante given to passing pedantic gas. He had a spine made of spaghetti and on the rare occasion one of our ideas advanced to Ablondi, this didn't mean it had Gillooley's endorsement. "I hate this," Ablondi would say.

"Ray," brave Bob would reply -- even though he had approved it this far -- "I couldn't agree with you more."

Day after day, Joe O'Donnell watched this charade, until he'd reached a boiling point. In a courageous -- if dangerous – gambit, he carried his concerns forward to Ford's relatively new marketing manager Lou Lataif and to Lataif's bosses Ben Bidwell and Phil Benton. "I don't like to go behind anybody's back" Joe told them, "but you deserve our best work and the people in your advertising department are not letting it get through."

Benton requested a summit meeting in New York with Don Johnston and Burt Manning. He said that yes indeed he wanted J. Walter Thompson's best work and, to that end, he was making changes in his advertising department. Their marching orders were to not interfere with the process. His promise of free rein came with a serious challenge.

"You'd better be good," he said.

Old Ablondi didn't go quietly. In fact, he didn't really go at all. He simply slid over to the position of Director of Market Research and began a concerted effort to waylay any creative work delivered to him for consumer testing. He became a turd in the punchbowl.

17
The Redoubtable McClure

Doug McClure's corporate roots ran deep. His father was an old-fashioned family doctor who delivered several generations of Ford offspring. When Doug achieved age, it seemed inevitable that he would join Ford and, when he did, he became one of Lee Iacocca's boys -- a group of hard-charging salesman who rose through the ranks on a very fast track. The upward course of his career effectively ended at the moment of his greatest promotion: to national sales manager for the brand new Edsel division.

Doug arrived as Ford's new advertising manager without personal agenda or ulterior motive. His open manner encouraged free and honest dialogue. He seemed to genuinely enjoy the give and take of advertising ideas, whereas Ablondi had made it a daily contest between our imagination and his lack of it. ("How can I visualize what I can't see?" Ablondi raged one day.)

For his part, Lataif greatly increased the intelligence level of the creative discourse. He had a quick mind, boundless energy and, fortunately, a sense of humor. When he began to meddle in our copy a bit too much, I bought him a large pen in the shape of a trout. Our rules were simple: he could make copy changes if he wished, but only if he used the fish pen. That pretty much ended that.

McClure and Lataif changed the temperature in the room and the serious work of rebuilding the brand began. It helped that there was an exciting new product on the horizon: the first of Ford's so-called "world cars." In the coming model year, Escort would launch the company into the modern era, driven by the front wheels. America responded enthusiastically and one couldn't help but be struck by the depth of residual good feeling for Ford, even though their loyalists had being fed a steady diet of stylishly bland, technologically deficient cars for more than a decade. It was finally time to put a couple of old shibboleths to their final rest – "Found On Road Dead" and "Fix Or Repair Daily."

But even with new advertising management at our backs, turning around the bottom-line culture at Ford would prove as difficult as turning around the Queen Mary at full steam. Like their kin at Chrysler and G.M, Ford was still a slave to the "Thirty Day Report." God have mercy on us if sales of the Chevy Impala inched ahead of the Ford LTD for a moment or a month. Taking the long view was not encouraged.

Ford had fallen into other nasty habits. Emphasis was always placed on features rather than benefits. "It's got a big trunk," national sales manager Bernie Krumpton would say between naps. "Tell 'em about the big trunk." And then there were the often misleading and always bothersome gas mileage ratings. The law required that, if you chose to advertise your mileage, you had to superimpose the actual MPG figures large on the screen – both highway and city – and to include a mouse-type disclaimer of at least three dozen words below. This effectively killed any possibility of image building or story telling. Even though communications research showed that most consumers tuned out the claims and disclaimers entirely, and, even if they took notice, didn't much believe them anyway, The Big Three persisted on pursuing their blind course. (The truth rarely mattered, here. One day, another of our crack account management team – Larry Mastro – raced back from Ford to order a hurry-up spot touting the fact that Ford had the best fuel economy numbers of any U.S. car company.

"Well, do we?" someone had the temerity to ask.

"No," Mastro said with oblivious conviction.)

And pity the fools who dared try to be creative. We once booked a choir to sing the tongue-twisting mileage disclaimer against the music of a Bach fugue. The good humor people at the Environmental Protection Agency were not amused and ordered us to cease and desist with such foolery.

Most grievous was the industry's continuing reliance on re-bates. Initially, rebates had been effective in boosting short-term sales, but they became less and less so with every succeeding one. Customers came to expect wads of cash back with every transaction. Suddenly, they were not out to choose the better car; they were out to get the better deal. (When's the last time anyone ever paid full price for a refrigerator?) The car business – once built on the thrill of freedom and the romance of the road – was turning into the appliance business.

"Lou, we've got to get off the dope," I said with rising frustration. "We've got to start inviting buyers to choose Ford cars on the merits rather than on price. BMW wouldn't do rebates." While Lataif might have agreed in his breast, he just couldn't intellectually bring himself to get off the rebate merry-go-round.

"Bill," he'd say back. "BMW has to sell 3,000 cars a week. I have to sell 30,000."

Contrary to Hollywood portrayals of the advertising process, big executional ideas just don't emerge out of thin air or arrive fully formed. Instead they are born from fundamental truths that often must be dug deep for, leavened by inspiration and the insight that only comes from experience, and allowed to simmer over low heat. By the time they burst into advertising, they are sturdy enough to stand scrutiny and brave enough to advance into new creative territory.

In the Detroit Ford group, we had come to believe that Ford owners were unique in their emotional attachment to the brand. They might not be able to explain why, but people truly liked their Fords. Even if they had a quibble with the current models, there was a Ford in their past for which they still held a fond affection.

Although it ran counter to the client's 1981 thinking, the name "Ford" clearly carried more meaning for owners than that of any individual nameplate. In a lapse of judgment, Ford had taken to running away from the maker's mark and chosen instead to emphasize individual car names such as Mustang, Thunderbird and Granada. They even went so far as to remove the Ford Oval from the Thunderbird for a year or two. "It's important to recognize," we preached in presentation, "that every car in our lineup has an invaluable first name."

Ford was at least a year away from introducing the full lineup of cars that would allow them – and us – to break things wide open. But the validation and acclaim of the Escort gave us air cover enough to begin transitioning into a new kind of Ford advertising – less detail and feature driven; more emotional and engaging.

Jerry Apoian gave these beliefs their first expression. "Look Out World," he wrote, "Here Comes Ford." Members of the client voting group found in that phrase a clarion call they could march around the table to, and we in the creative group found room to run with a more uplifting message. Dan Hughes designed a unique print look with silver as a distinctive fifth color. ("I don't like it," Gillooley said.) We featured cars in bright colors to make them jump from the page. Let BMW and Mercedes dress in gray and black. We were going to be fun and outgoing and drive the brand younger. Jimmy Thomas, Larry Carroll, Bert Markland, Dick Howting and Rik Gloff helped lend each of the car lines a human personality.

The campaign suggested music and I placed a call to Paul Hoffman in New York. Paul, once road manager for the Edgar Winter White Band, was among the new breed of jingle producers, schooled in the rock and roll age, able to transfer their pop sensibilities to thirty-second and sixty-second tunes. I had met Paul during my final days on Kodak and we'd established an immediate and firm bond. It was a personal friendship and business relationship that would endure for a quarter century.

In those days, the prospect of landing a major car account was like winning the lottery for a jingle company. Producing and arranging fees plus performance residuals could run annual incomes for writers and singers into easy six figures. Often, such large accounts were won after lengthy, demeaning, and ultimately resource-draining competitions. As a creative director, I followed a decidedly different philosophy: pick people you feel will best serve the client, challenge them to do their best work, demand their total commitment, and reward them with your loyalty and your business. If their performance was ever found lacking or their commitment anything less than total, mine was always the plug to pull.

"Paul," I said. "Could you fly to Detroit tomorrow? I'll buy your ticket and you can bunk at my place." Paul arrived at the Detroit office soon after midday. He met the group and they took him through the "Look Out World" print campaign and some first television ideas.

That night, after Paul and I had returned from a late dinner, I put two glasses and a bottle of Dewar's White Label in the middle of my living room coffee table. "Tonight we figure out the Look Out World song," I told him. "We don't sleep until we know what it wants to be."

Even after we had sketched out the basic form of the song, we had no idea of just how important a role it would play as the campaign evolved. During the next few weeks, Paul's 23rd Street studio and Broadway's Automated Sound would become my second and third homes.

18
Greenies and Bloodies

The New York jingle business in the 70s and 80s was a 24-

hour-a-day hustle -- a hurly-burly of song pluggers, session gypsies, tomorrow's stars and yesterday's heroes. Everyone in the game seemed to have touched the fringes of fame -- from Paul's copyist Phil Medley, who'd written *Twist and Shout* for the Isely Brothers to keyboard player Paul Shaffer, destined to become musical director for *The Late Show* with David Letterman. The session singers on the date might have just rushed over from laying down backing vocals for Steely Dan. A couple of Blues Brothers were likely in the band. Mr. Fabulous. Blue Lou. It was intoxicating.

If you ran a jingle company, your success was determined by the talent you could attract and inner group you could assemble around you. That Paul Hoffman could attract and assemble anyone was, on the face of it, absurd. Paul had never taken a music lesson in his life and couldn't tell a minor fifth from a slide trombone. But he had an impresario's touch, a producer's ear and an unerringly infectious groove. He could find a distinctive lick for every one of the 48 multitracks at his fingertips. "Fill 'em all, Paul."

If you happened to be walking along the south side of West 23rd in 1981, you might have heard Paul Hoffman music coming through a 4th story window. I'd shown up to work with Paul and his composer-in-residence, Steve Benderoth. In those days, Benderoth was doing most of his composing beneath a Panama hat and behind a florid face suggesting controlled substances. (The last time I saw Steve; he was standing in the middle of 6th Avenue at 2: 00 in the morning – in his Panama hat -- directing traffic. They took him away soon after that.)

From the beginning, a shared conviction guided our days. We weren't going to write any old advertising ditties. We were going to break new ground with personality-focused, hook-driven road songs.

The journey proved more difficult than we anticipated. How in the name of Elton John do you devise a single song structure with the melodic glue to hold the whole Ford lineup together from car to car, yet give each model fresh air to breathe? LTD was comfortable and middle aged. Mustang was hot and street smart. Escort was family and functional. EXP was unmarried and sporty. To us, Fords were not about horsepower and trunk space. They were all about life stage and mindset.

Members of Paul's inner circle made their presence felt. A collection of prodigies and pros, they shared an ability to change musical colors with the facility of chameleons. The chief orchestral arranger was David Wolfert, a Grammy and Emmy nominated composer who was also a pop songwriter of considerable note. (He counted Dolly Parton, Whitney Houston and Barbra Streisand among his covers.)

It's hard to overstate the spiritual force that was Frank Floyd. Frank was the unofficial godfather of New York session singers – those gifted nomads who bounced from studio to studio for four, six, eight recording dates a day – singing about laundry soap in the style of Aretha Franklin one moment and about breakfast cereal a la The Monkees the next. No matter who was in the group, Frank would take command of the vocal booth, sound out the harmony parts and, when things were going all to hell, keep these insanely talented creatures from breaking out of the asylum. (Frank taught me an important early lesson: session singers have an uncanny ability to read lips. Even out of earshot you dare not

103

express the slightest discouraging word lest you bruise an easily offended vocal ego.)

While he worked all around town, Frank was becoming more and more a fixture at Paul's, helping out with the writing, singing rough demos, and righting our course if we headed in a wrong direction. "You can't sing that word, Bro," he'd say to me. "No, no, you can't sing that." As life played out, Frank would be our godfather for the next quarter century.

Kurt Yaghjian was a cliché. He arrived at the Port Authority Bus Terminal in February 1971 with a few bucks in his pocket and a tenor that could reach the balcony. Within days, he had sung his way into the original Broadway cast of *Jesus Christ Superstar*. But Broadway shows inevitably close and the choice new parts have a way of going to the next just-off-the-bus boy singer. To pay the rent, Kurt fell into Frank's orbit of session singers. Kurt and Frank. Frank and Kurt. It became so that you would rarely see (or hear) one without the other.

"Orlando! Como está, bro?" Paul tipped Orlando a twenty for the bag of Bloody Marys and Heinekens he'd just delivered to Automated Sound Studios. It was about 8:00 in the morning of a busy writing and recording day and it was certainly not the last time we would see Orlando before the sun went down. (Or, for that matter, before it came up again.) After a week of frustrating fits and starts trying to get the Ford song "in the pocket," I'd ordered a dozen or so "Ford Concept Team" satin tour jackets and gave them out to the recording engineers, singers and key musicians. We must have looked like a bunch of rock 'n roll roadies, but it gave a signal that everyone's opinion mattered and everyone's help was needed. As Ford's Phil Benton has warned us upon granting us our creative freedom, "you'd better be good."

A nervous Joe O'Donnell was flying in from Detroit for the session. Manning threatened to stop by.

As fortune would have it, backbeat and syncopation came to our rescue. We began to place the lyric rhyme and the metric stress at the second-to-the last word of the line instead of at the end -- which is more expected:

Even Got a HATCH Back
Pretty Tough to MATCH That

By the time O'Donnell arrived at 10:00 p.m., the band was in the studio, our handpicked collection of session singers was assembled, and we had four songs to sing. Lani Groves arrived from a record date with Ashford and Simpson. Of course, Kurt and Frank were there. Gordon Grody showed up in a gold lame jumpsuit and co-opted an equipment dolly to glide across the room – just as O'Donnell showed up. Joe looked at me and raised an eyebrow. I shrugged my shoulders and turned my palms to heaven. Nothing out of the ordinary in Jingleland. "Orlando!" Paul shouted, as another bag of greenies and bloodies was delivered.

History will report that *Look Out World* fell into pocket that night (*Pretty Tough to MATCH That*) and that the campaign suddenly took on a life of its own. O'Donnell exhaled. "You'd better show Manning where you're going," he said. So the next morning, with nervous ears, I played the tracks for Burt. (Anyone who worked for him in those days will tell you about the dangers of playing Burt vocal tracks. He simply couldn't hear a good mix. "Make the singers louder," he'd say. "Yes, sir," we'd say, and create a special "Manning Mix," just for him. "That's it! That's it!" he'd say. Then, we'd go back and do it the way we wanted to anyway.)

Burt did a small jig. "You don't even need a storyboard," he enthused. "I can see the pictures in my head."

Even though we had been promised that those in the Ford advertising department were going to "stay out of your way," courtesy obliged us to show them what we were up to. Doug McClure and Lou Lataif were quick to see (and hear) the power of *Look Out World*. Predictably, Bob Gillooley proclaimed the music "just a lot of noise." Bernie Krumpton couldn't find a big trunk anywhere. Our commercials were dramatically unlike anything they had seen.

We scripted two full-fledged musicals for Mustang, based on the most popular movies of that summer. *Fame*, starring Irene Cara in a story about the School for the Performing Arts, had made movie musicals cool again. We cast Irene to make a cool musical for us. *Nine to Five* was an infectious tale about secretaries gaining the upper hand on their bosses. We restaged that with a starring part played by a Mustang Convertible. In our creative universe, Escort became a friend of the family and the sporty EXP went to a rock concert featuring the group of the moment, Air Supply.

The New York Ford group was leaving us pretty much to ourselves. They busied themselves doing truck advertising, which had always been kept separate from car. We thought we finally had them in our rear view mirror.

Manning had other ideas.

19
In the Horseshoe

On a top floor of the Glass House, where the brothers Ford still sat, the elevators opened to armed guards. Down a hallway wide enough to accommodate a car, and off to one side of the Ford boardroom, was a small, windowless office into which representatives of the J. Walter Thompson Company were ushered one nerve-wracking day in 1981. They lugged large black portfolio bags containing Ford advertising plans for the upcoming fall new-car introduction.

With shined shoes and a healthy case of nerves, I found myself waiting in that small office -- for what seemed an eternity -- with JWT Chairman Don Johnston, Burt Manning, Joe O'Donnell and Jerry Apoian, there to lend moral support and to help with presentation choreography. We would have two hours to offer our insights on the current market situation to Ford's top management, and show them creative work in layout and storyboard form. Don would make an opening statement; Burt would do the market setup, and then yield the floor to me.

We were shown into a boardroom the size of an airplane hangar. The board table itself was at least fifty feet long and shaped like a horseshoe. A small army of Ford executives, including Lou Lataif and Phil Benton, greeted us. After we had all settled into pre-ordained chairs, Benton announced that Chairman Philip Caldwell would be arriving late and that we should go ahead and begin.

At our request, several easels had been strategically arranged inside the horseshoe. A small stereo system with two good speakers was positioned within easy reach. Burt pulled several large foam-core boards from one of the black bags and used them to bullet point his market analysis. (Alas, no PowerPoint in 1981.)

As I walked to the end of the table and through the opening of the horseshoe, I was reminded of what Joe had told me. "Once you step inside," he said, "you're on your own. If you get in trouble, nobody will come to your rescue." I was well into my part when Caldwell entered through a door at the head of the table. All rose. Caldwell turned to Johnston and, with due respect, greeted him warmly. While Ford President Don Peterson was positioned directly to Caldwell's right, the seat on the left was reserved for Don. And so the ritual went, with Manning and O'Donnell given honored places next to their appropriate Ford counterparts. "We don't need to go through the set up again," Ben Bidwell said. "Bill, why don't you begin from the start of the creative presentation." Manning was miffed that he didn't get to perform his part for the chairman, but this was not his boat to rock.

I worked without notes. Moving closer to Caldwell, I talked about the enormous reservoir of good feeling towards Ford that existed across the land and about how this was just the moment to tap into it. "People are tired of rebates and bad news," I said. "It's time to proclaim a new day for the American car. Who better to lead that charge than Ford?" Jerry walked to the stereo and pressed play. A sixty-second anthem version of the *Look Out World* song filled the room. While it played, I reached into a black bag and pulled out the first of the oversized print ads Dan Hughes

108

had designed, this one featuring a bright red Escort. Caldwell leaned forward and asked if he could hold it at close range. In the next few moments, Jerry and I lined easels with giant silver print ads, each featuring a brightly colored Ford. Soon, Caldwell was fairly surrounded by Escorts, EXPs, Mustangs and Mustang GTs.

We had prepared separate music mixes for the different commercials. In each, the lyrics were dropped out at designated points to accommodate announcer copy. In presenting a concept, we would first walk through the scenario using larger-than-life "gloryboards." Then, as the appropriate version of the song played, I read the copy live, fitting the announcer parts snugly between vocal choruses.

As we took Caldwell and company through each carline, they followed intently, never missing a note. At the end, Johnston gave a thoughtful summation and asked if anyone had comments or questions. "It's thrilling," Caldwell said. You've given us all great hope." As he rose to leave, we all rose, too. When the door closed behind him, there was a momentary pause, then a great spontaneous buzz, bordering on applause. In the midst of it all, Phil Benton – Ford's Division General Manager, and the one who had said to us "You'd better be good" – stood on his chair and asked for quiet. Turning to Don and Burt, and then to me, he said: "Thank you for saving my job." I had earned my chips.

Our greatest challenge lay ahead. In little more than two months, we would have to present a dozen or more finished commercials at the annual kickoff meeting in Las Vegas – a raucous little affair that officially begins the new model year. *Look Out World* would face 5,000 of Ford's severest critics – their very own dealers – buffeted in recent years by inferior product, increased foreign competition and almost continuous profit-sapping rebates. Tough crowd.

For all intents and purposes, the creative group abandoned Dearborn for the duration. Producers Jerry Apoian and Larry Carroll headed west to shoot Escort, LTD and Thunderbird in the California countryside. I headed east to shoot Mustang on the streets of Manhattan. After Director Steve Horn finished principle photography on *Fame* and *Nine to Five*, we shipped his film to L.A. and followed it there for editing and postproduction.

We made headquarters near the Universal lot, where Editor Howie Weisbrot had set up shop for the summer. (Howie had been cutting Ford car commercials for more than twenty years and had been through this dealer-show drill that many times before. The term "warhorse" comes to mind.) But a rather ugly issue suddenly arose. Like many in the Detroit group, Jerry Apoian felt that Howie was beholden first to the New York creative group and would not give Detroit spots his full loyalty and commitment. Jerry suggested we cut with Jim Edwards at an editorial house called Ace & Edie in Hollywood. We agreed on a compromise: I would continue to cut with Howie; Jerry would cut with Ace.

Music men Paul Hoffman, David Wolford, Frank Floyd and Kurt Yaghjian flew in from New York to begin laying down basic tracks at Evergreen Sound. We not only had television to do, but a music-driven radio campaign. Over the next few weeks, Neil Sedaka would sing Escort and Air Supply would serenade the EXP; Tanya Tucker would do a Mustang tune and Tony Bennett would croon for LTD.

As deadlines approached, twelve-hour days stretched into sixteen-hour sessions, which morphed into twenty-hour marathons. I bounced from Howie to Ace and back to Howie again, looking at rough cuts, laying down announcer temp tracks, screening dailies of new spots just coming in. Not that there wasn't time for debauchery. Bars nearby would stay open late, knowing we'd be there eventually. Frank and Kurt were spied cruising around Hollywood in a rented Jaguar convertible, usually in the company of fetching women, never the same two from day to day.

One night, because he'd never been there, I invited Mike Priebe to the Beverly Hills Hotel's Polo Lounge for a late drink and, hopefully, some celebrity sighting. The place was jammed as usual, but I had come to know the maître d' well and he squeezed us against a banquette across from the piano. Priebe found himself sitting next to David Susskind, a pioneering talk show host and famous face, in a B-list sort of way.

"You're an old fag," someone called out from the next table. We looked up to see a very drunk man who was directing his comments at Susskind. "D'ya hear me? Just an old fag." When he excused himself to go to the men's room, the woman he was with came over to apologize to Susskind and to us, who just happened to be sitting in the vicinity.

"He's really not like that," she said. "He's a writer for Carson and has been under a lot of pressure and…" At that moment, the drunk returned. Thinking that Priebe was hitting on his girl friend, he coiled his arm as if to throw a punch. Suddenly, the drunk was on the floor – his arms pinned behind his back – being dragged unceremoniously out the door. I suspect that this was a bit more celebrity than Priebe had bargained for.

In the final week before the dealer show, the post-production process went on around the clock. Both Evergreen studios – A and B – were booked full time for recording final tracks. Voice-overs and final mixes were made in the middle of the night. Howie and Ace had Pacific Title on 24-hour call. Hollywood's film labs readied the final 35mm show reel. For someone like me going through it for the first time, it was a marvelous thing to watch.

Flying home the next night – well and thoroughly exhausted – we looked down on the lights of Las Vegas and crossed our fingers.

20
The Man with a Satchel

Clever copywriting and innovative art direction can only perfume a pig for so long. So, it's safe to say that Ford would not have enjoyed the mid-80s resurgence it did without the innovative leadership of its president, Donald E. Petersen. Petersen called Joe O'Donnell one day in early 1982 and asked if he might visit the agency to meet with key JWT people. He demanded absolute secrecy, so Joe secured a windowless conference room on the creative floor.

Petersen arrived by himself – no aides, no staff, no Ford

marketing men in tow. He carried a small black satchel and placed on the table in front of him. The doors were locked. "A few years ago," he began, "I held a meeting with our designers and engineers and asked them if they were proud of the Fords they were parking in their driveways. When they said they were not, I asked why?"

The designers and engineers laid the blame squarely at marketing's feet and, most particularly, on their slavish adherence to the opinions of consumer focus groups. (Focus groups, for those who have never been in one, are comprised of demographically selected citizens willing to give up an entire evening for twenty-five bucks and a ham sandwich.) By the time Ford brought to market the cars that focus groups said they wanted, it would be five years later, tastes would have changed and Ford would find itself five years behind again.

These sentiments were echoed by none other than Henry Ford II, who still threw his weight around the Glass House. "We got into a frightful habit in this company of relying too much on surveys," he told an author writing a corporate history. "I think that if you are in the business, you ought to know what the hell you want to do, and you can't rely on a survey to pull your bacon out of the frying pan."

"I told the designers to trust their own instincts and to create the cars they had always wanted to," Petersen said. "I challenged the engineers to build these designs for quality and operational integrity – not just for cost efficiency." He reached into his satchel and, one by one, extracted small-scale models – one, two, three, four. They were unlike any designs we'd seen – what would become known as Ford's "jellybean" cars.

"These are the best cars we know how to build," he said. "Our job is to make them." He turned to me. "And your job is to make people like them." Clearly, now was not the time for messaging that recalled past campaigns -- or to promise that the "future is right around the corner." The new theme should reflect the pride and confidence of a maker introducing a whole new generation of automobiles.

When it comes to developing a theme line, the key to success can usually be found in a single word – a powerful, surprising, unexpected word – one that holds up a traffic sign and compels an audience to stop and think. If Panasonic's theme of the moment had simply been "Ahead of Our Time," it would have been largely ignored and quickly forgotten. But "*Slightly* ahead of our time" made the thought resonate and stick. We kept that lesson in mind as we fought through the process of arriving at a theme position for the new Ford. We instinctively knew that it couldn't be a brag. People would simply not stand for being told that Ford was better; they would have to conclude it for themselves.

During one of our creative barnstorming sessions, we were messing around with the notion of issuing a challenge when somebody uttered the words "When was the last time you drove a Ford?" We all sat up. It was half of an idea and we began tossing it around. Suddenly, soon-to-be familiar words fell into place – including a final one that would make the line famous -- and "Have you driven a Ford lately?" was said out loud for the first time.

From its first expression, *Have You Driven* blew every other line off our wall and we began developing executions around this singular thought. As it always does, we knew music would help seal the deal; lift the notion; provide the emotion. So I began to call in all my resources to write this critical tune. Of course, Paul Hoffman would be involved, but, first among others, I asked Roger Nichols if he wanted to compete. (Roger had just composed ABC TV's new Olympic Theme and, since I thought *Have You Driven* wanted to be big and anthem like, full of brass and percussion, he seemed a logical choice.)

I flew to L.A. to work with Roger. As always, he rose to the challenge, I wrote a lyric and we cut a full orchestral demo. I was convinced that we already had our tune, but I owed Paul a chance and caught the redeye back to New York – managing to catch the flu along the way. I checked into the Plaza Hotel, sick as a dog, and slept for most of the day. Finally, I called Paul and told him I thought we already had the song and that I was going home to Detroit. "C'mon, Bro," he said. "We've got something great. You gotta give us a shot."

I took a cab to the 23rd Street studio about 5:00 and found Paul on his way out the door and Frank Floyd sitting on the floor – with a ukulele. "Be back in a sec, Bro. Listen to Franco." Listen to Franco, sitting on the floor with a ukulele. Jeezus.

Frank begin to pluck and sing. *Have You Driven a Ford* (plink, plink, plink, plink, plink, plink, plink), *Then You Must Be Very Happy* (plink, plink, plink, plink, plink, plink, plink), *Have You Driven a Ford* (two, three, four) *Lately*? Of course! The spaces between the notes. Along the way, we would have to get rid of the "Must be very happy" line and the ukulele, but now you know that it was Frank Floyd who added the three magical dots that completed one of the most memorable car themes in memory:

Have You Driven a Ford...Lately?

It took me less than half an hour to craft a complete lyric:

> *When Was the Last Time*
> *You Had a Car Like This to Drive*
> *Talking About the Kind of Car*
> *That Brings the Road Alive*
>
> *Remember When*
> *How Long Has It Been*
> *Put the Key in*
> *Put Your Foot Down*
> *Let It Go*
> *You've Got That Feeling Again*
>
> *Have You Driven a Ford*
> *Then You Don't Know What You're Missin'*
> *Have You Driven a Ford...*
> *Lately*©

Over the decade and a half of its existence, *Have You Driven* commercials would be sung by dozens and arranged a thousand different ways. But, early on – even in demo form – the song found its one true voice in Kasey Cysik. Opera trained, and having enjoyed a measure of popular success with the original movie recording of *You Light Up My Life*, Kasey's pure soprano became indelibly identified with Ford. Over the lifetime of the campaign,

Ford estimates that her voice on *Have You Driven* was heard by a cumulative audience of more than 20 billion people. (Tragically, Kasey's life was cut short by cancer in 1998, when she was only 44.)

Surprise. As we went about busting our gut developing the most important campaign for Ford in its recent history, we heard rumors that New York had been asked to do a campaign, too. The source of the request is still uncertain. It could have come from Ford (Ablondi was still lurking around in his new role as head of marketing research.) It could have been Manning, who always seemed to be hedging his bets. All we knew is that, once again and this time unexpectedly, we were locked in a pitched battle with our own agency – a contest that would unnecessarily drain our resources, sap our energies and ruin our weekends. *Have You Driven*, we were to find, excited the Ford people, but frightened them at the same time. It was neither traditional nor literal. It didn't speak to gas mileage and big trunks. There was no chest beating or boast. One spectacularly misguided point of view thrown in our path was that no proper theme line should contain a question. "What if someone says "no?" they said.

Well, we were in for the final fight. We had assembled a team that I knew was up to it. We certainly had the right idea on our side, but sometimes the good guys don't win. And what if, after all we had built here in Detroit, the creative pendulum swung back the other way? What message would that send to the group, the Detroit advertising community and to Ford?

21
The Y.F.C.C.

"We're fucked," Dick Howting said to no one in particular. "Manning's going to take that New York campaign and ram it right up our ass." The group was about to gather in a little alcove right outside my office to discuss the latest news and to make war plans. This common space came to be known as "Club Bobo."

During the coming days of around-the-clock creating, Le Club would be the collection zone for all manner of scatological messaging, much of it scathing, none of it printable. It provided blessed relief from what seemed like endless internal meetings, countless client presentations, and frequent visits from Manning. It would also cause continuous acid indigestion for Joe O'Donnell and the other responsible adults on the 3rd floor.

During working weekends, Bobo became the Y.F.C.C. "What's that stand for?" I asked innocently.

"My friend," Howting said, "you are sitting in the You're Fucked Country Club. O'Donnell and Balestrino are out playing eighteen holes of golf and we're stuck in this dump."

Of course, cocktails were involved. Dick had acquired a duplicate key for the back door of O'Donnell's office, in which Joe maintained a full and well-stocked bar. After hours, Howting would let himself in, pilfer two or three bottles, and open for business at Le Club.

There were days when lunches went a little longer than they should have. It was Good Friday and I was on the phone with Manning when I heard a car horn honking wildly. I looked out my window to see Howting's orange Volvo perched – no, stuck – on the crest of the berm separating the JWT parking lot from the street. Inside the car, Dick and the Doc, just back from a martini or two at Giullio's, calmly smoked until they could be rescued by two mystified men in a tow truck.

The New York group was pulling out all the stops, calling in every creative chip they'd collected over the years. It seemed the entire supplier industry – from jingle houses to film production companies to Hollywood talent agencies – had chosen sides and was betting on one or the other of us to win, obviously in anticipation of a big payday should they pick the right horse. (The most egregious example of pandering occurred when one of the talent groups provided New York with the voice of Sir Sean Connery – for free – to intone these immortal words: "Ford. It's for you." Shakespeare this was not.)

We were dancing a strange dance. In a move bordering on desperation, New York put forward a campaign based on their long-running "Built Ford Tough" truck positioning. Manning grabbed onto this idea as if it were the Holy Grail. In his literal-minded way, he believed that "tough" would equate to "quality" in the consumer mind. Anyone who had been paying the slightest attention to reality knew this was like trying to sell shotguns to the PTA. The audiences for trucks and cars are totally different. You may drive "tough" to the construction site, but you certainly don't drive it to the church picnic.

Meanwhile, the Detroit group stood bravely by *Have You Driven*, gladly taking on all challengers. We spent our days defining car personalities (according to their audiences), refining executions and honing messages.

Jim Thomas and Burt Markland created an indelible image for Escort. Their conceit was that Escort is the ultimate "back and forth" car – a virtual metronome of everyday living. To the train. Home from the train. To school. Home from school. To hell. And back. The visuals were always left to right, right to left. The ultimate takeout was that the Escort was the most reliable car in America. Genius.

Larry Carroll and Rik Gloff provided muscle for Mustang. "Let's not talk about the wimpy secretary Mustang," Larbo would say. "Let's boss up." One of their spots was conceived to be shot in the steel forges of the River Rouge. Their *Have You Driven* music tracks were hot, hot, hot. "Mix it in the red, Paul, mix it in the red!" (Later that year, when the boys stopped by the office at the end of the forge shoot, they looked as if they were about to perform a blackface routine in a minstrel show.)

Dan Hughes and I met late one night at Beau Jack's, a burger and beer joint a couple of blocks up the road from where labor boss Jimmy Hoffa had been kidnapped. We were under the gun to come up with an introductory campaign for the new Thunderbird – very definitely a jellybean car. Totally smitten with its looks, we decided that the less we said, the better. So we said nothing. Dan grabbed a pile of cocktail napkins, and in a technique that hadn't been used before (but has been much imitated since), we created a campaign that had no announcer – only a few words, scattered in super throughout the thirty seconds. For the first spot, I wrote: "If...we...didn't ...dare ...make...it...different... we...wouldn't...dare ...call...it...Thunderbird." (Some in the Ford advertising department didn't believe this had a hope in hell of working. So, at Gillooley's insistence, we made an animatic for testing. "Dare" scored higher – and by a wide margin – than any commercial they'd tested before.)

Ford must have enjoyed the spectacle of the agency fighting with itself, believing, in some perverse way, that this constituted maximum service. So, New York and Detroit made a number of joint presentations to succeeding levels of Ford management, each level passing the decision buck up the ladder to the next. Along the way, it became evident to everyone but Manning that *Have You Driven* was the clear favorite and that the client was just waiting for JWT management to stand behind it. The only way New York could win was for our campaign to be killed outright.

Ray Ablondi intended to do just that. As the director of Ford Market Research, he fielded a consumer study in cahoots with "independent" pollster Marty Goldfarb – in fact, an old crony of the New York group. He was to present his findings at a very large meeting of senior decision makers, chaired by Ford Division General Manager Phil Benton. Before Ray delivered his report, Benton asked me to present the work one more time.

Ablondi stood and walked to an easel, which held a number of large charts. He proceeded to cite "evidence" that *Have You Driven* was absolutely the wrong campaign for Ford. First of all, he maintained, questions never make for successful theme lines. Benton turned to me. "Well, Ray," I said, "what about 'Wouldn't

You Rather Have a Buick?'"

"But that's a question that can only be answered by a 'yes,'" he said confidently. "If we ask people 'Have You Driven a Ford Lately,' they'll likely say 'no.'" Benton looked at me again.

"What's the next question, Ray? Did you ask them a second question? After they say 'no,' what's the next thing they say? Here's what they say, Ray. They say 'no – "but maybe I should.' That's what they say, Ray."

What happened then can only be described as a total career meltdown. Ablondi began to fume and sweat and babble that his research was proof and that none of us had the slightest idea what we were doing. After an awkward silence, he was escorted from the room.

That year's big meeting with the Chairman was scheduled for very early in the morning and I can remember getting dressed in the dark. In the green room – just before we were to enter the horseshoe – Manning walked over to me with a sartorial observation. "Bill," he said, "don't let this distract you, but you're wearing one black shoe and one brown shoe." I hurriedly borrowed a matching pair from one of the account men who had carried over our set-up boards. And so, before the Chairman of the Ford Motor Company, I presented *Have You Driven a Ford...Lately?* in Dennis Sinclair's shoes.

The production schedule to get ready for the big dealer show was no less strenuous than in years past. We had to shoot, cut, score and finish fifteen spots. Again, Paul Hoffman Music relocated in force to the West Coast and took over both studios at Evergreen. Jim Edwards, the "Ace" of Ace & Edie, was editing everything now and averaged no more than three or four hours of sleep a night over the last two weeks leading up to the show.

We didn't fly over Las Vegas that year with our fingers crossed. In fact, we attended the opening session in which the new campaign was to be introduced. The lights dimmed and the first bars of *Have You Driven* came over the sound system. Jerry Apoian had created a sixty-second film that previewed the entire campaign. By the time Kasey Cysik hit the chorus, there were 5,000 dealers on their feet, stomping and cheering.

As it turned out, *Have You Driven* ended up running for fifteen years. In consumer surveys, it is by far the most recalled car campaign of the last half-century. It was inspired by Don Petersen and the tiny model cars in his black satchel; brought to life by Frank Floyd and his ukulele; threatened by competing forces within J. Walter Thompson itself; and almost single-handedly killed by Ray Ablondi on his way out the door.

From that time forward, anyone who spied me driving home at night in my Mustang – and happened to glance at the license plates – could figure out, without too much trouble, what I did for a living. The plates simply read: "LATELY."

22
Bill & Kinder's Excellent Adventure

If you'd run into Kinder Essington at the local A&P, you never would have suspected he was a first-rate creative man. He walked around the halls of the Little House with a look of detached bemusement, running the General Accounts creative group with benign good nature. He owed his physique to his father Tubby, who had strutted his way to a certain notoriety as drum major for the famous Ohio State Buckeye Band.

Reared in Grosse Pointe, Kinder grew up on the other side of the tracks from the Firestones and Fords. That bothered him not at all and he regularly crashed the Ford kids' extravagant parties by hot-wiring a car along the way. When he felt the urge to go home, he simply hot-wired another car and went back across the tracks to the Essington side.

Kinder withstood the incessant needling of the arrogant bastards in the Ford group with remarkable aplomb, earning their grudging respect in the process. On one notable occasion, Howting arranged a wine and cheese event for the General Accounts group to celebrate their slew of recent Caddy Awards, Detroit's equivalent of the Clios. When everyone had assembled in the conference room, Howting clinked his glass to make a toast.

"The Ford group would like to congratulate you for winning all those Caddys. The way we figure it, the revenue from General Accounts for a whole year is less than we added this week with our latest Ford rebate campaign. Drink up." Brie and epithets flew.

I'd recently been elevated to Executive Creative Director of the Detroit Office and, charged with overseeing the entire creative operation, had grown to know and appreciate Kinder's management style. One way or another, the notion arose of him crossing the border to the Ford side of things. When his knees momentarily buckled at the thought, Joe O'Donnell gave him a swift kick and over he came.

In the course of Kinder's introduction to the ways of Ford, I invited him to New York to sit with Manning and me in one of our monthly creative status meetings. As we landed at LaGuardia, we noticed a few flakes of snow beginning to fall. By the time we reached 466 Lexington, the city was in full blizzard. We learned after the meeting that all area airports were closed, and would be into the following day. Fortunately, the Grand Hyatt – which happened to be a Thompson client – squeezed us into their fully-booked hotel. We settled our brains for a long winter's nap, resolving to rise early the next morning to make our way home as soon as LaGuardia opened for business. Wishful thinking.

"They say the airports may not open until tomorrow." It was Kinder on the phone and it was 7:00 in the morning. I suddenly felt the warm glow of mischief wash over me.

"It's a lost day, Kinder," I said. "If you're of such a mind, we might get ourselves into some trouble."

"Well, I could use a Bloody Mary."

"I know just the place."

In the bowels of the pre-Jackie Kennedy, grungy old Grand Central Station, tucked behind the Vanderbilt stairs, was a saloon that always smelled like last year and opened as early as the law allowed. At 7:30 a.m., Kinder and I were not its first customers. In fact, we had to wait our turn for a place at the bar. From that perch, we watched a parade of dirty little secrets in gray flannel suits, just off the New Haven from Rye, stopping by before work to slug down a quick drink or two. Kinder's eyes went wide.

We had the good sense to have breakfast before setting off on our next adventure, which required the impossible good fortune of finding an available taxi cab and a willing driver and then negotiating the relatively unplowed streets of Manhattan. I played a hunch and led Kinder to the Hyatt's rear entrance, the one up

125

where Park Avenue detours around the Pan Am Building. Aha! An empty cab. The rooftop sign said "Off Duty," but I figured the cabbie might just be using that as a defense against someone who wanted to go where he didn't want to take them.

"I'm off duty," he said.

"Do you know where McSorley's is?" I said back.

"It'll cost you twenty, he said." The meter was off.

McSorley's Old Ale House, down on 7th Street in the East Village, is the oldest pub in New York. Abe Lincoln had a mug or two there, as did Boss Tweed and Woody Guthrie. It was the last bar in America to permit women, which it did by court order in 1970 and which old timers will tell you ruined the place. McSorley's staged its own form of stout Irish protest by not installing a dedicated ladies room for another decade. It's no more than a mile from Grand Central as the crow flies. But there were no crows flying that day, and, in these conditions, it might as well have been in Wyoming. We'd start down one street, only to have to double back the wrong way to escape a stranded snow plow. Zigging and zagging southward for what seemed like an hour, we eventually spotted McSorley's in the snowy distance. An hour is a long time to spend in a taxi without talking and, soon enough – invited or not – the cabbie joined our conversation. No, he had never been to McSorley's. Yes, he'd like to go someday. No, I can't drink while I'm driving. Well, maybe I could have one beer.

The row of buried cars in front of McSorley's discouraged parking. No matter. The cabbie simply rolled up onto the sidewalk and parked there -- next to a fire hydrant. Once inside, one beer turned into two and two to ten. (Actually, McSorley's serves only light and dark ale of its own making, and you must order them

126

two at a time.) After a plate of stale cheese and raw onions, Kinder and I sent a rather tipsy cabbie on his way – but not without a back slap of accidental camaraderie and a souvenir McSorley's mug.

Once or twice during the morning, we called Detroit to check in on happenings there. Oh, my. Important meetings had been postponed because of our absence and the account people were all asweat. Their palpable angst was salted with token sympathy. "You poor guys," they sighed. "You must be bored to death." Little did they know that we were prancing around Manhattan like Bialistock and Bloom in *The Producers*, playing hooky from the daily grind and enjoying every damned minute of it.

We ducked into the Astor Place subway station, our next destination being Pete's Tavern on Irving Place, one stop north. As Kinder headed for the bar, I brought him up short. "No, no. You must sit over here." It was important, I thought, that he enjoy his beer in the very booth in which, during one cold winter's week, O'Henry had written *The Gift of the Magi*.

And so the day went. I showed him the long-preserved Thurber cartoons drawn on the barroom walls of what once was Tim Costello's in midtown. We left enough eating room for a celebratory steak at the original Palm, long the unofficial dinner club of New York's newspaper fraternity.

As midnight approached, the snow had stopped, but its aftermath had scared all but the bravest cars off the streets. Ignoring the wisdom of sidewalks, we strolled back to the Hyatt right down the middle of Lexington Avenue.

"How 'bout a nightcap," Kinder said.

"I know just the place."

23

Beneath the long shadow cast by the automobile industry, there is a surprisingly rich texture to Detroit, generationally deep and culturally complex. Whereas New York City collects drifters and dreamers from the far reaches, Detroit is a born-here, die-here town. Family counts, relationships matter, friendships endure.

And history resonates. Detroit's most famous native son, the great heavyweight Joe Louis, might have been long gone, but down in a sweaty, musty basement, the Kronk Gym continued breeding future champions such as Tommy Hearns and Evander Holyfield. Barry Gordy might have taken Motown to Hollywood and Vine, but up on West Grand Boulevard, you could still visit the original Hitsville, U.S.A.

We hired two young copywriters who echoed that culture and history. Bill Leonard was the son of hometown author Elmore Leonard of *Get Shorty* fame. Harvey Briggs' grandfather had been the long-time owner of the Detroit Tigers, and Briggs Stadium stood in eponymous tribute at the corner of Michigan and Trumbull.

Detroit was knit tight in many ways. In New York, most senior advertising executives flee to the suburbs at the close of business and, as a result, social hours lack the sense of true community. In Detroit, foes by day are often friends by night. One is reminded of British and American generals during the Revolutionary War who, after the sun had gone down on battle, would meet at the local roadhouse to share brandies.

Illustrative is the evening I happened to be having dinner at the Fox & Hounds with Dick Macedo, an old friend just assuming the top account job at Campbell Ewald on Chevrolet. "Mind if we join you?" I looked up to see Ben Bidwell, who had recently become president of Chrysler. With him was Glen Fortinberry, the head of one of his major agencies. And so we broke bread together: The creative director of JWT on Ford, the account director from Campbell Ewald on Chevrolet, the president of Chrysler and the CEO of Ross Roy. Only in Detroit.

JWT became part of the downtown scene late in 1982 when Ford "invited" us to abandon the Little House on the Prairie and to take up residence in their Renaissance Center. It was about that time that a couple of new recruits to McClure's group made our lives rather more interesting. In an effort to train them in all aspects of the family business, the Fords dispatched their only sons to spend a year learning about advertising. First through was Henry's son Edsel, who turned out to be a perfectly delightful colleague, in spite of his father's historically dismissive opinion of J. Walter Thompson. ("Edsel," I said to him one day, "I'd like to meet your father. Could you introduce me?"

"Lane," he said after a moment's thought, "not even I could pull that off.")

Next to fall into our irreverent clutches was William Clay Ford, who was immediately dubbed "Billy Ray," and suffered his schoolyard name with remarkable equanimity. Little did we (or he) know that within 15 years, Billy Ray would become Ford's Chief Executive Officer and, eventually, its Executive Chairman.

With the instant notoriety of *Have You Driven* and at Edsel's urging, Thompson became more and more involved in community affairs. We began to work closely with Mayor Coleman Young, who asked us to help him persuade residents from the outer suburbs to make downtown a dining and recreation destination. To our chagrin, the mayor fancied himself quite the copywriter and came up with his own campaign theme: "Do It In Detroit." We advised him that this might be problematical in light of Detroit's reputation as the murder capital of the United States and home to a vast underworld of drug pushers and prostitutes. He dismissed all such talk and said, "Write me one of those good songs of yours. We'll get the Four Tops to sing it."

"Hello, Paul," I said. "We've got a new gig." Off I went to New York and we wrote the city a love song – certainly not called "Do It In Detroit." In keeping with the mayor's intent, we wrote a very Motown/Four Tops tune called *Be a Part of the Heart of Detroit*. It was introduced with much fanfare at city hall, the mayor presiding and the Tops performing live. We were front page in the Detroit News the next day. And, unfortunately, the day after that. I had been interviewed by the News and asked why the song was called *Be a Part of the Heart* when the mayor's theme was "Do It in Detroit."

"Frankly," I said, a bit impoliticly, "we were afraid of the obvious and not very flattering double meanings."

Oh, my. A headline the next day screamed "Mayor and Copywriter in War of Words." I had blundered badly over a classic stimulus and response situation and had considerable crow to eat. Thankfully, the mayor accepted my apology with grace and good humor. And a wagging finger.

As I approached the end of my fifth year in Detroit, I began to get itchy. O'Donnell had been transferred to Chicago to take over the JWT operation there. Balestrino had just been appointed manager of the San Francisco office, and Markland and Gloff followed Chuck to the Bay Area. The Ford account was, for once, humming along smoothly. Kinder had settled into day-to-day oversight nicely. I got the feeling it was time to go.

So I flew into New York to chat with Burt Manning. Suddenly, I was a problem he hadn't foreseen and didn't need. "This isn't an ultimatum," I tried to reassure him. "And I'm not in a hurry. I just want to know what the Company thinks my next move might be. I don't choose to stay in Detroit forever." What I didn't tell him was that I'd been recruited by agencies on both coasts for executive creative director posts. One offer was from the largest agency in Seattle where I would also have a 25% ownership position. The other was from old friend Gerry Broderick of Kodak days who had just become CEO of Arnold Communications in Boston and wanted me to join him there.

But, even though these might have been nice lifestyle moves, they ultimately seemed like backward steps to me. I had recently been elected to JWT's U.S. Board of Directors and was enjoying the challenge of dealing with broader Company issues. I frankly enjoyed the big stage of J. Walter Thompson and wasn't ready to go back and play summer stock.

Events conspired in my favor. When Balestrino and Gloff got to San Francisco, they found a creative department in disarray. Apparently, the situation was so dire that they called in Manning. Burt asked them what they would suggest. They suggested me.

I was completely unaware of all this, so Burt's call came

from out of the blue. "How would you like to be our creative director for the West Coast?" he asked. Evidently, he had some concerns about the creative output in Los Angeles, so he asked if I would oversee both offices. It didn't take me long to make up my mind.

And so, I began to wean myself from the creative group I had built – of which it could be said, built me -- and the clients I had grown to respect – true friends all. Ford was kind enough to host a goodbye party at the Renaissance Club. Part toast and mostly roast, it was a boozy, wonderful evening. The final speaker was Edsel Ford, who presented me with a vintage Seeberg jukebox filled with Motown records. In my remarks, I repeated a long ago request.

"Before I leave Detroit, would you please introduce me to your father?"

Edsel stayed true to character. "Not a chance, Lane," he said, at the microphone and for all to hear. "Not a chance."

Part III

24
The City

It was around the time of Ronald Reagan that American culture began to tilt west. Youth-driven pop music, which traditionally bubbled up from the bayous and boroughs east of the Mississippi, found a new wellspring in California. In San Francisco, Carol King, the Shirelles – and the Brill Building gave way to Grace Slick, the Grateful Dead and the Fillmore Auditorium. *Rolling Stone Magazine*, the Holy Bible of the rock era, was born across the Bay as a counterculture tabloid. Beat poetry found a permanent home at the foot of Telegraph Hill in the City Lights Bookstore, where proprietor and patron Lawrence Ferlinghetti was threatened with jail for publishing Allen Ginsberg's "Howl." The Hungry i and the Purple Onion in North Beach introduced us to the brash new comedy of Mort Sahl, Lenny Bruce and George Carlin. Bob Hope, Red Skelton and Uncle Miltie they were not.

As the culture drifted west, so did the soul of advertising's creative revolution. The eastern ethnic voice that for a generation had supplied us with humorous and award winning campaigns for Volkswagen ("It's ugly, but it gets you there"), Alka Seltzer ("I can't believe I ate the whole thing") and Levy's Bread ("You don't have to be Jewish to love Levy's"), gave way to the folksy charm of San Francisco's Hal Riney. It was not only Hal's writing, but also his voice we heard on Reagan's famous "It's Morning in America" campaign film – the one that propelled the Gipper toward his Presidency. Back East, advertising spokesmen had traditionally taken on the wise guy personae of Joe Isuzu or FedEx's

133

"Fast Talker." Instead, Riney gave us two down-home codgers named Frank Bartles and Ed James sitting on their front porch dispensing wisdom about Gallo wine coolers. While Pepsi and Coke battled toe-to-toe over who could sing the biggest jingle, Riney gentled us with "The Earth's First Soft Drink" for Perrier. New York advertising was insistent and in your face. San Francisco advertising was laid back and took its time.

Almost all the major national agencies had outposts in San Francisco. BBDO had long served the Standard Oil Company of California (now Chevron). Foote, Cone & Belding had a creative reel that featured ground breaking music-video commercials for Levi's and the famous claymation "California Raisins." While Y&R and Ketchum also had strong footholds, it was the hot creative shops Goodby Berlin & Silverstein and Chiat/Day that, along with Riney, drew the most national attention and defined what came to be known as "the San Francisco school of advertising."

As the 1980s dawned, there was a new buzz around town. An historical confluence of technological advances, entrepreneurial spirit and a vigorous Reagan economy ignited the computer age, with its epicenter just down the Bay in Silicon Valley. Overnight, San Francisco agencies were awash in high-tech accounts that attracted a whole new generation of advertising people eager to ride the leading edge. This army of young professionals, their pockets suddenly filled with spending cash, made the City its playground.

And the City opened its arms. Up and down its seven hills and around just about every corner, new neighborhood bars with names like Casablanca and Company came alive with testosterone and romance, cheerfully coexisting alongside tradition and history.

A big advertising hangout was Reno Sweeney's in the Embarcadero where, on a given evening, you could expect to see an elegantly dressed Joe DiMaggio. You never approached Mr. DiMaggio for an autograph or a conversation. No, no. You learned to leave him alone with his highballs and his memories.

If you worked near the financial district, you might hang out at the House of Shields, a turn of the century drinking establishment that only recently had removed the spittoons from the brass foot rails of its massive redwood bar. (Shields had a decidedly different atmosphere during another part of the day. It happened to be located just across the street from the offices of the *San Francisco Chronicle*, the City's leading morning newspaper. After working a long, dry night, the press people were well thirsty by dawn. Our five in the afternoon was their six in the morning and Shields was their bar.)

In San Francisco – no matter what the generation – civility held its own. As in Paris, there seemed to be flower stalls on every corner. My father remarked that it was the last city in America where women wore gloves. And even if that wasn't quite the case anymore, you could still visit the Top of the Mark or the decorous Cirque Bar at the Fairmont where the crowd came dressed to the nines and hewed to the old manners.

There was mystery down every alley. The ever-present fog made the pavement eternally wet and shiny, which only added to a certain noir sensibility for those who walked its streets. You learned to stay away from the societal dark areas like the Panhandle, a homeless haven where too many runaway youths ran into too many drugs. And, in this postcard-perfect, tourist-infested place,

135

one learned to avoid this element, too. Cable cars, Ghirardelli Square and Fisherman's Wharf were best left to visiting firemen.

J. Walter Thompson had been a San Francisco citizen in good standing since 1923. Future JWT CEO, a precocious Norman Strauss, got his start there and, if you trust the written-down history, "introduced the 'bleed' technique to newspapers and helped develop-run-of paper, full-color advertising."

In later times, Thompson San Francisco was defined by Harry Lee, who joined in 1936 and acted as manager from 1955 on into the 70s. According to my colleague Ridge Lundwall – who had gone through the process – Lee was noted for asking every candidate for employment: "In times of crisis, do you turn to Jesus Christ?"

As politically incorrect as his question might have seemed at the time, its implications must have resonated in 1980 San Francisco. The City had become the national focal point for a frightening new disease. Although there were rumors and suspicions, nobody yet knew exactly where it had originated or had proof of just how it was passed along. More alarmingly, there was no hard science on how to prevent it from spreading. The common belief was that it was essentially a gay plague, and in this climate of fear, City Supervisor Dan White murdered homosexual activist Harvey Milk, taking out Mayor George Moscone in the same fusillade. White's conviction for manslaughter – and not murder – galvanized the gay community and resulted in the culturally devastating White Night Riots.

The disease had San Francisco scared stiff. They called it AIDS

.

25
Panty Palace

To call the San Francisco office in 1984 a loosely run or-
ganization is to give it too much credit. It had a general manager
who wasn't given the authority to manage, two creative directors
who couldn't direct traffic, an artist named Hogg, a writer named
Heaven, and an entire account group that routinely went to lunch
together and not so routinely came back.

After years of humming along nicely with a few solid accounts of its own, as well as acting as a field office for the Ford
Dealers Association, the explosion of high tech had made San
Francisco suddenly and accidentally robust. Who knew that the
Southern Pacific Interstate Communications Corporation would
turn into Sprint, spending like a Russian heiress to compete with
AT&T and MCI for the long-distance dollar? Or that quiet, re-
spectable Hewlett-Packard, which had built a tidy little business
developing precision measuring devices, would become a major
force in this new frontier called personal computers? The burgeon-
ing category of video games delivered Activision to Thompson's
doorstep. And, when the first computer retail chain opened for
business, JWT invited people to "Make Friends with the Future" at
ComputerLand.

As I arrived, my good friend and San Francisco's nominal
general manager Chuck Balestrino was trying to swim to Alcatraz
with one arm tied behind his back. Counter to its usual common
sense, Thompson had saddled Chuck with Jim Agnew, who, in ad-

dition to his role as Los Angeles general manager, carried the title of "Manager of JWT West." Throwing his titular weight around and sporting a lifestyle befitting his lofty self esteem, Agnew kept a beautiful company apartment on Nob Hill (which came to be known as Panty Palace) and could be counted on to spend one or two days a week occupying the San Francisco manager's office, dispatching Balestrino to an anteroom next door. A social creature by nature with exceedingly white teeth and a firm handshake, Agnew knew next to nothing about the inner workings of our accounts, but was always good for hosting a long lunch or an expensive dinner at one of San Francisco's finer restaurants. His constant courting of our senior clients effectively cut Balestrino's balls off.

JWT/Chicago had contributed two creative directors to San Francisco: Mac Churchill and Charlie Martell. Each had enjoyed success in their past professional lives (according to legend, it was Charlie who created the ingenious "Un-Cola" campaign for Seven-Up), but neither displayed the slightest talent for leadership.

Mac had hired most of the creative group and "Mac's guys" owed a certain loyalty to him. He pretty much let them run their own show and they seemed quite satisfied in their collective mediocrity. The only ones Mac hadn't hired were Bert Markland, Rik Gloff and me – referred to, dismissively, as the "Detroit mafia." Along with Chuck Balestrino, we were regarded as glorified grease monkeys – and, as such, rather boorish, unclever and crude. Gosh.

Mac kept a half-gallon bottle of vodka in the credenza behind his desk, ever poised to spill a healthy shot into a waiting coffee cup. Early in my stay, I happened into his office at about 8:30 in the morning – just before a new business presentation. He was "rehearsing his ad libs." As we rose to go into the presentation, Mac reached behind his desk and poured a shot. He slugged it down, turned to me and winked: "Show time!"

But even though ill led, Thompson had its share of the young leading-edge group that was reinvigorating the rest of San Francisco; who more than made up in spirit and desire what they lacked in experience. In time, they would form the core of a more directed – if not disciplined -- JWT San Francisco.

Within a fortnight of my arrival, Hewlett-Packard fired JWT. After the fact, Rik Gloff traveled to Palo Alto with Clyde Hogg to make a creative presentation, but was interrupted half way through. One client turned to another and said: "Don't they know?" No, they didn't.

Activision went away soon after that. It typified the new breed of high-tech companies evidently born without the ethic gene. These companies didn't much like the traditional agency 15% commission system and set about breaking its back, replacing it with their own arbitrary payment structure. "Take it or leave it," they would say. "We can always find another agency who will work for less." They could and they did.

ComputerLand was a slightly different case. Just before Chuck was appointed general manager, account director Roger Lewis presumed that he was in line for the job. Unfortunately (according to those who were there), Roger made an unfortunate speech at the annual JWT Christmas party after one too many eggnogs, offended almost everybody, and was invited to leave the company the next day. Ominously, Roger popped up soon after as ComputerLand's advertising director. One day, we received a call from one of the major art studios in town. They had completed several storyboards for ComputerLand commercials and wanted to know whom they should deliver them to. We scratched our heads. We hadn't ordered any storyboards. But, apparently, BBDO – at Roger Lewis's direction – had. Bad manners, bad omen, bad end to our relationship with ComputerLand, which met its own demise soon after.

Our Silicon Valley bubble burst as rapidly as it had artificially inflated, which had unfortunate consequences. Chuck Balestrino, through no fault of his own, had "gotten behind the management curve," as they say. Even though he'd been instrumental in winning the Dole and the Diet Center accounts, the loss in quick succession of the core of Thompson's high-tech business proved too much to survive in the corporate world. The Company removed him to Tokyo to handle Kodak/Japan. (Not too many years later, Chuck would return to JWT/Detroit and become a very successful general manager there.)

Thompson acted quickly to replace Balestrino. A long-time general manager named John Florida was imported from Mexico City. At first glance, John seemed to be a good fit. He had major-office management experience and had been schooled in The Thompson Way. But, looking back, I should have regarded Florida with some skepticism. During his stint in Mexico City, he brought in my old partner Mike Millsap as creative director. It wasn't long before word of political unrest drifted my way. "Florida's a fool," Millsap told me over the phone. "We're trying to get the work right and he's running around acting like some banana republic dictator, paying off the police to get his parking tickets fixed."

Knowing Millsap, I just thought he was harmlessly venting. But not long after, Florida fired Mike for insubordination, froze his assets and held him virtual prisoner in his own house. Millsap may have not been an innocent in all this, but the whole sordid matter seemed a bit off.

Bad times had given me an opportunity to do a bit of creative housecleaning. Mac and Charlie were among the first to go. Hogg and Heaven followed soon thereafter. Mac made a particularly dramatic exit. Already boozed up before lunch, he chose the occasion of a weekly management meeting chaired by Florida to read a long diatribe against everyone and everything at the agency. After dousing a half-smoked cigarette in his vodka-laced coffee, he taped his resignation to John's door and left JWT/San Francisco forever. Displaying a creativity he rarely did on the job, Edwin Heaven returned to his office after hours, set the trash on fire, sooted up the walls, and proceeded to sue JWT and the Embarcadero Center for faulty ventilation.

The Chevron team, dysfunctional as it was, should be given some credit for their ability to handle the infamous advertising director Herb Hammerman, who reigned terror from that post for the better part of three decades. Hammerman made an odd appearance – gnomish, portly, his hair parted down the middle, and his suit coat (always on) buttoned at all three buttons. After agency meetings, where morning pastries had been served, Herb would linger, scoop whatever pastries remained into a napkin, and conceal them in his briefcase.

But questionable pastry behavior doesn't begin to describe his taste in advertising. When reviewing the work upon first arriving in San Francisco, I was greeted by a cringe-making spot featuring service station attendants dancing on the keys of a giant cash register. Hammerman thought this was the bees knees, telling me with a straight face that "it's best thing we've done in years." My stomach churned.

While it lasted, Dole was great fun. President Rick Wolfort treated the agency as a true partner and took advantage of the full range of resources we could provide. At times, unfortunately, we put his trust to the test. In bidding out a print photography assignment, art director Rory Phoenix recommended shooting a print ad in the Caribbean – this for a client whose headquarters (and identity) were in Hawaii. "The water is bluer," he claimed. Rick bought this argument hook, line and South African accent. (By the way, after traveling all the way to that far off sea, Rory ended up staging the scene in a swimming pool.)

Everything was going along, ahem, swimmingly until Rick's board of directors shot the company out from under him and sold it to land baron David Murdoch, who decided that "we need to go in another direction" on the advice of his new marketing director H.R. "Bob" Haldeman – yes, the very same.

The San Francisco client that presented the biggest challenge (and the biggest upside) was Sprint. This was at the very dawn of the telephone wars – ignited by the government's breakup of AT&T – which threw the long distance category open to anyone with deep pockets or a gambler's stake. It also helped if one were an interstate railroad, with thousands of miles of roadbed along which to install telecommunications wire, telephone switches and multiplexing equipment. To handle complex communications between its engineers and dispatchers, Southern Pacific had established a vast long-distance network independent of the Bell System. This "Switched Private Network Telecommunications" mouthful became the acronym "Sprint."

In the beginning, AT&T was such a dominant power that Sprint regarded MCI as a more realistic competitor and price as its primary selling point. Though Sprint's and MCI's service was shoddy and their quality iffy, consumers flocked to these new carriers in expectation of saving a bundle. The problem was, they tended to flock away just as fast because of a lousy product experience. The daily challenge was to see which company could dump the most new users into the top of their customer funnel while keeping the fewest old users from spilling out the bottom.

San Francisco had been running a nice little campaign called "Straight Talk" Cleverly written by copywriter Rachael Gilday and shepherded along by associate creative director Jim Sanderson, it won a couple of awards and everybody on both sides of the agency/client table seemed to like it fine.

When I was introduced as the new executive creative director to Sprint, they asked me how I liked their campaign. "Where's the 'and?'" I asked. They looked at me as if I'd just flown in from Mars -- or, well, Detroit. "Everybody knows you've got low price," I said. "Everybody knows MCI has low price. The game will go to the one who gives the customer something in addition to price. What's your 'and?'"

While this question mark continued to hover over Burlingame, Sprint seemed content to stay merrily on their current course – until MCI fired a shot across the bow. MCI's marketing director, a good ol' boy from "Nawth Ca'lina" named Ed Carter came up with a program called "Friends and Family." Deviously simple, it rewarded customers with cheaper rates on calls to those closest to them – if these friends and family also joined up with MCI. As a result, customers became recruiters, too, and a single core person could bring in a dozen others.

None of us knew it at the time, but life was about to radically change for the folks at Sprint. And Ed Carter would have a lot to do with that.

26
Knock Down Drag Out

J. Walter Thompson made a stunning announcement at the beginning of 1986. Don Johnston stated his intention to step down as only the 5th chief executive officer in the 125-year history of the Company and to nominate Joe O'Donnell as his successor.

O'Donnell was a surprising and, as it would play out, fateful choice. Though his track record in Detroit and Chicago was impressive, Joe had no international experience, long regarded as an essential rung on the Thompson management ladder. Don intended to stay on for a year or two as chairman of JWT Group to allow Joe to travel the world and get a feel for the often-arcane nature of JWT's international operations.

As an inevitable consequence, Burt Manning abruptly resigned, seeing his path to the top of the Company blocked by the young and vigorous O'Donnell.

In his first months on the job, Joe certainly didn't need any crises at home. Alas, San Francisco handed him a beauty. Communications giant GTE, which had swallowed up little Sprint and operated it out of California as GTE Sprint, now joined in 50/50 partnership with a small but extremely capable Kansas telephone company called US Telecom. They declared war on AT&T as US Sprint and, in the same breath, announced an immediate account review. It was only fair, they said. After all, US Telecom had a very good agency of its own – the powerful Chicago office of Foote, Cone & Belding – and they certainly wouldn't need two agencies going forward. So, both existing agencies would be given an equal opportunity to compete for the entire account. It would be David vs. Goliath.

A briefing was scheduled in Chicago for late February. Senior United Telecom executives would address Foote, Cone in the morning and Thompson in the afternoon. Not to be out-Goliathed, JWT brought in its biggest gun, O'Donnell himself. General manager John Florida and I led the team from San Francisco.

When Joe was delayed due to weather, Charles Skibo, the senior executive representing United, asked each of the rest of us to introduce ourselves, present our credentials and make an opening statement if we wished. As the briefing began, O'Donnell burst through a door at the back of the room, visibly upset, and took a seat next to Florida.

"Mr. O'Donnell," Skibo said. "Welcome and would you like to say something by way of introduction?"

"I'd like to say," Joe said with an edge to his voice, "that I think you might have had the courtesy to wait for the president of the J. Walter Thompson Company before beginning." Uh, oh. I could see our client sailing right down the river with Joe's ego on board.

For their part, United Telecom put on a deep and thorough presentation. As one of their engineers spoke, I made a note. "Eventually, we intend to make Sprint a completely fiber-optic network," he said.

When it came time for questions, I asked the engineer: "Why, exactly, is this fiber-optic thing so important? What does it mean to the average Joe?"

"Fiber optics will deliver ultimate transmission quality; better than consumers have experienced before. Have you ever been on a call so quiet that you have to ask the person on the other end if they're still there? We call that 'drop-dead sound.' You're on fiber optics."

San Francisco went to the mattresses. Our very survival hung in the balance. The Thompson Company's chief strategic thinker, Bert Metter (yes, that Bert Metter, who had been creative director for the New York Ford group), moved into our offices and began to develop a platform for the presentation. We quickly homed in on fiber optics, not knowing if Foote, Cone had caught the same drift during their briefing. One thing baffled us: If this technology was so advanced, why didn't AT&T have it? Or MCI, for that matter? It took Bert a day or two to come up with the obvious answer: they couldn't. Both AT&T and MCI were much bigger than Sprint and it would be prohibitively expensive for them to go completely fiber optic anytime soon. By the accident of its size (and thanks to an influx of capital from United Telecom) Sprint was small enough to make the move.

I gathered the core creative team. Jim Sanderson had been one of the most loyal of "Mac's boys." Still, in this moment of crisis, he managed to stuff his allegiance in a drawer and work for the common cause. Steve Weiss, Debbie Lawrence, Rory Phoenix and Paul Cuneo were relieved to be out from under Mac and Charlie, and eager to buy into the new order. Even though they were still regarded as outsiders, Bert Markland and Rik Gloff were invited to pitch in. In addition, I had just recruited writer Mike Gallagher and was in hot pursuit of art director David Bigman – using much the same strategy as I had in Detroit. I asked Weiss, who knew almost every creative person in the City, to identify those around town who had the talent and temperament to make a good fit here and, most importantly, might be seduced by the opportunity. No hesitation. Gallagher and Bigman.

"Forget everything you think you know about Sprint," I told them. "Forget every campaign and every execution we've ever done – no matter how successful." Sanderson gulped. There went "Straight Talk." I went on and on about fiber optics and of the colorful language the engineer had used to describe its effect.

"How do we communicate the concept of 'drop-dead sound?"

The presentation was scheduled for April Fool's Day. To get a feel for our office and staff, United Telecom would come west for the meeting. As D-Day drew closer, everybody involved was working around the clock – except for a curiously disengaged

John Florida. It seemed that John enjoyed the trappings of being a general manager, but didn't relish getting his hands dirty with client business – certainly not after five. I wasn't the only one who noticed.

We suffered momentary second thoughts when reviewing our approach before a strategic review board of senior Thompson executives, assembled to question and advise. "What if fiber optics doesn't happen right away?" asked Don Sullivan, general manager of JWT/Chicago. "What if it's an over-promise? Shouldn't we have a backup position?"

After an hour's debate, O'Donnell weighed in. "Look," he said, "we're way behind going into this thing and we need to impress them right out of the box. Fiber optics is their only story – and ours, too. Throw long."

Of course strategy is critical, but in new-business competitions, it's inevitably the work that carries the day. We had winnowed our campaigns to three. The first was very announcement oriented. It's always wise to have an "at last, it's here" execution in the bag, if only to fan client egos. Our "it" was AT&T and the astounding notion that "America's Going to Have the World's Best Telephone Company -- Again." How dare little Sprint challenge gold standard AT&T? How dare, indeed.

But, we devoted most of our creative attention to the other two: a demonstration concept and an emotional one -- both focusing on fiber optics. The group had concocted all manner of intriguing ways to address drop-dead sound. One featured an operatic soprano who hit a sustained C-above-C that broke a glass at the other end of a fiber–optic line. Another had Stevie Wonder recording a bi-coastal duet via fiber optics. And Sanderson came up with a silly little mnemonic to symbolize quiet: a pin drop.

I had written the theme for the third campaign. Not surprisingly, I'd taken a less-technical, more-emotional approach to drop-dead sound. The engineer's description of the experience of speaking on a completely noise-free line had stayed with me. When I experienced it myself, I said, as most people do: "It sounds like you're right next door."

Charles Skibo headed the client team from Kansas City, where Sprint headquarters would be relocated. His manner was courtly and he spoke slowly, with a slight drawl. To his right was Big Ed Carter – the bombastic man from Nawth Ca'lina – who had invented "Friends and Family" for M.C.I. Ed would serve as Sprint's director of marketing as they moved forward.

Metter's strategic setup set the trap for drop-dead creative.

"This is your moment," I began. As usual, I spoke without notes. "For Sprint's entire life, the subject has been price. As Ed surely knows, it's a game anybody can play, but nobody wins. Now, it's time to change the subject – and Sprint is the only phone company that can do so."

"For the first time in history, Sprint can attack AT&T where nobody has before: On quality." In ad after ad, campaign after campaign, we laid out the case for quality. At a crucial moment, a speakerphone in the middle of the conference table rang. I invited Charles Skibo to push the answer button. It was Stevie Wonder – who, via prior arrangement, talked about how he would pull off his bi-coastal recording.

As expected, the client raised the key question. "You know," Skibo said, "our network is not going to be complete for some time. How do we get around that?"

"Consumers will give you credit for beginning," I said, trying not to sound too glib. "If you say 'we're building the first and only fiber optic network in America – even though it's not completed – they'll play along with you. And when you say to them 'wait 'til you hear it,' they'll keep trying until, one time, they'll actually get a call that's on fiber – and then you have them for good."

The next day, John Florida's secretary caught me in the hallway. "Bill, somebody's on the phone in John's office and he thinks you should take the call."

"Hello, Bill." It was a soft drawl. "This is Charles Skibo and you oughta know y'all kinda knocked our socks off the other day. If it's all right with you, we would be proud to have J. Walter Thompson as our agency. Oh, and one other thing: Do you suppose you could write us a beautiful theme song?"

Within minutes, Scoop Kapsiak, our A/V guy, had located Wilbert Harrison's recording of "Kansas City" and was piping it through the agency. Suddenly, there were 120 cheering bodies gathered in the conference room – 120 tired but happy souls who soon found themselves on the Tiburon Ferry for a party at Sam's, a dockside bistro up the bay and across the Golden Gate. It was a defining moment.

The party lasted until the wee hours and Sam's likely set a house record for drinks served in a day. Showing his true Irish, Gallagher got into a fight and was escorted from the premises. On his way out the door, Mike put his UCLA hat on David Bigman, who, during the party, had accepted our offer to join the Company. A few moments later, the police arrived and were told to look for "the guy in the UCLA hat!" Alas, it wasn't the rogue Gallagher they arrested, but the unsuspecting (if not entirely innocent) Bigman.

A late call that night informed me that Bigman had been booked for drunk walking.

27
Flowers from Hal

Like almost everyone else, I wandered into the office a bit late the next morning, Sam's having done me in. When I did arrive, a large bouquet of flowers sat on my desk. I opened the card: "Congratulations. Thanks for keeping the business in town, (signed) Hal Riney." The unexpected Sprint victory was a win for the whole San Francisco advertising community – for the art studios, production houses and all the unsung, below-the-line companies that owe their very being to local agency success.

It wasn't a time to rest on laurels – especially not where Big Ed Carter was concerned. He was anxious to get started right away, so account director Steve Sanchez, management supervisor Sherry Carniglia and I found ourselves on a plane to Kansas City before week's end. (In the mid-80s, the only way to fly directly from San Francisco to Kansas City was on the dying wings of

TWA – whose letters, according to comedian Freddie Prinze, stood for "Try Walking Asshole.")

We were to discover that a meeting with Carter the next day was always preceded by a dinner the night before, where Ed would hold forth on subjects ranging from Kansas City barbecue to those dumbass Congressmen in Washington to the roadhouse at the edge of his property in North Carolina he'd just bought and renamed. "'Twas Red's," he announced. "'Tis Ed's."

Carter redefined the meaning of two-fisted drinker. As we sat down to have barbecue that first night, Ed immediately ordered two bourbons. He placed one near his right hand and one to his left. That way, as he gesticulated his way through the conversation, there was always a glass near whichever hand was free at the moment. As one glass emptied out, the waiter would immediately replace it with a full one.

Apparently, Charles Skibo had been serious about me writing a song for Sprint, so, instead of going back to San Francisco, I headed to New York and Paul Hoffman. Along with the ever-laconic Steve Tubin (Paul's latest composer-in-residence) we wrote a big power ballad called *Right Next Door* and conceived it as a boy/girl duet. As this would be our first chance to impress the new client, we recorded a full demo with a 30-piece orchestra and I flew back to Kansas City to play it for Charles.

"I'm afraid we really don't have much audio/visual equipment," his secretary said. "But I do have my daughter's boombox." I wasn't going to play our new tune for Skibo on a boombox, so I looked for equipment-rental services in the Yellow Pages and ordered a sound system to be delivered immediately and set up sooner. By the time Charles returned from a long lunch meeting, his office looked like The Bottom Line. We blew his ears away.

For air, *Right Next Door* was performed by Michael McDonald and Kim Carnes, but not without incident. After agreeing to terms, we set a date to meet at Evergreen Sound to lay down final vocals. While Kim cooled her heels in the studio, Michael remained in his limousine and dispatched his manager to deliver a new demand. "Since Michael's a bigger star than Kim," the manager said, "he feels he should be paid more."

I picked up the phone and called my friend Rick Hersh, an agent at William Morris, which represented McDonald. "Michael is sitting in a car outside about to renege on our deal," I said. "I've booked the time and my client is sitting in the control room without any idea of what's going on. If Michael isn't in this studio in five minutes, I'll write a memo to every creative director at Thompson worldwide and recommend that they cease engaging William Morris artists until further notice." A well pissed-off Michael McDonald walked into the studio five minutes later and sang his ass off:

We're a Thousand Miles Apart
And Yet I Still Can Hear Your Heart
And I Know You're Not So Far from Me Anymore

From a Half a World Away
I'm Hearin' Every Single Word You Say

153

As If You Had Been Sayin' Them from Right Next Door
It Sounds the Way that Love Should Be
So Close That I Can Almost See
Your Voice Come Smilin' Back at Me
It Sounds Like You're Right Next Door

Suddenly I Hear
The Way You Feel
Suddenly You're Near
And All at Once It's Real

It Sounds the Way that Love Should Be
So Close That I Can Almost See
Your Love Come Smilin' Back at Me
It Sounds Like You're Right Next Door

As is often the case in new business, a client will become infatuated with more than one campaign. So, even though it was agreed that the overall theme would be "Sounds Like You're Right Next Door," several of the demonstration commercials were approved for production. Indeed, the soprano's C-above-C did break the crystal glass. "And, what about that Stevie Wonder one?" Ed asked. "Can it be done, or were you just blowing smoke?"

Yes, it could be done. All Sprint had to do was run a fiber-optic line from their nearest network junction directly into Wonderland, Stevie's studio in downtown L.A. If Stevie's duet partner were in a similarly equipped studio in New York, it would be as if both artists were recording in the same room, singing into the same microphone. "Let's go talk to Stevie," Ed said.

And so began a particularly bizarre episode in "The Life of Carter," this new sitcom we suddenly found ourselves in the middle of. We flew to L.A. and arranged to meet Stevie at Wonderland on a mid-week evening about 7: 00. As 7:00 turned to 8:00 and 8:00 to 9:00, I was assured Stevie was in the building. His assistant pulled me aside, winked, and said that Stevie was momentarily occupied." I smelled perfume. Meanwhile, Ed and I were invited to occupy ourselves by drinking beer and shooting pool in the game room.

"Hi, Ed." Stevie Wonder came into the room and walked directly to Carter and shook his head warmly. I stood back and watched in amazement as this blind-from-birth ghetto kid from Detroit shot pool and the breeze with a Carolina cracker from the Deep South.

On our way out the door, Ed asked Stevie for an autograph. The assistant appeared with a piece of sheet music and an inkpad. Stevie made an imprint of his right thumb on the page – his official signature.

The quietest idea we presented on save-the-business day turned out to make the most noise – much to our surprise. Jim Sanderson had written a concept called "Pin Drop." To be honest, we really weren't all that excited about it. Setting up sensitive microphones to capture the sound of a pin dropping over a telephone line frankly didn't make the blood rush much. But, during production, Rory Phoenix reworked the script a bit, and gave the spot a sense of childlike wonder. We found a studio with a camera that could shoot the pin falling at twenty-five hundred frames per second. (Film is regularly shot at 24fps. Twenty-five hundred fps can follow a bullet fired from a gun.) We experimented with a hundred sounds to see if we could find the perfect one to play as the pin landed.

As it turned out, the pin falling was mnemonic enough. And for a decade, it ended every spot as Sprint grew from brash upstart to major player. They became the "Pin Drop Company." The consumer had voted. Stimulus and response.

As all this was going on, reality intruded. A male secretary in the media group went home early one Friday afternoon with a bad cold. On Monday morning, we learned that he had died over the weekend. Not long after, a young man in the traffic department, who had undergone a noticeable loss in weight, asked to work from home until "I feel better." He died the next week. The word around the office was that both had had AIDS. We had a mild panic on our hands. One group of employees formally petitioned to have the restrooms on one floor be designated as "gay only." We dispatched our head of human resources, Maureen Kazarinoff, to an AIDS seminar being conducted by Levi-Strauss for San Francisco businesses. After attending, she reported back to the management committee on the need to provide medical and psychology counseling to all who requested it and so we did. As knowledge was gained and information replaced rumor, a measure of calm was gradually restored.

But as that crisis began to quiet, another rose in its place. One day, John Florida received a bomb threat over the phone and we had to suddenly evacuate the office. The next week, another bomb threat forced a second evacuation. After a third threat, we called in the San Francisco Police Department. They conducted interviews and asked about possible disgruntled ex-employees and several fingers pointed to Clyde Hogg. His voice was easy to distinguish and no matter how he tried to alter its timbre, his uncommon speech pattern made his vocal identity evident. The problem was, we could prove nothing. And, unless we could, the SFPD could do nothing.

So we bent the law a little. We hired a beefy ex-cop, now working as a private detective. He placed a wiretap (illegal) on Hogg's line, and we caught him red handed. A visit in the night, a knock on his door, a gruff accusation, and Clyde Hogg was heard from no more.

An already memorable year was about to become infinitely more so. "How soon can you get back to New York for a day?" It was O'Donnell on the phone.

"What's this about?" I asked.

"It'll wait 'til you get here."

I figured that, whatever it was, it might carry a certain importance. So I made an appointment with my regular barber to get a haircut.

"Peter's not here," the boss barber said when I arrived.

"But I made an appointment," I pleaded.

"Peter's not here."

Peter had just died. I learned later he had AIDS.

28
A Change at the Top

In the culture of J. Walter Thompson, the position of general manager was sacrosanct. As a rule, managers were selected with care, installed with ceremony, and operated with the unquestioned imprimatur of the Company. While there was no handbook for general managership, and no crash course in practices and procedures, a new manager had most certainly been steeped in the Thompson Way and groomed by mentors at every turn. That given, he was expected to find his own footing, set his own course, and lead according to his own vision.

The only measure of success was success – success in maintaining strong relationships with current clients and growing revenues through additional assignments; success in increasing billings through new client acquisitions; and success in becoming a respected member of the community. The Company gave a manager goals; how he reached them was his business.

It was no secret that San Francisco had been for some years an office in turmoil, due largely to the Company's missteps at filling the manager position. The unfortunate Balestrino had been placed there without portfolio, his ultimate downfall pre-ordained by the overlording Agnew. John Florida – who had seemed promising on arrival – had proven to be clueless and ineffective. Still, nothing prepared me for what Joe O'Donnell was about to say.

"You seem to be running things out there anyway," he began, "so, we figure you should have the title, too. We'd like you to become general manager of San Francisco." "We" included Jack Peters, Joe's designated Number 2, who I'd known as account director on both Kodak and Ford. While Jack's loyalty, toughness and intelligence were never in question, he had the unfortunate habit of opening his mouth at just the wrong moment and sticking his foot in it. At Ford, there had been an explicitly stated "Peters Rule": while JWT was free to have anyone they wished sit atop the account, and as account director, Jack was free to attend any meeting, he was never – never – allowed to say a word.

To be honest, I wasn't sure about this general manager thing; in fact, I was decidedly unsure. A creative man by training, it was in that area that I felt I could bring a client the most value. Besides, I was totally unschooled on the bottom-line business skills it takes to successfully run an office.

Despite my protests, Joe and Jack didn't seem particularly concerned and asked me to get back to them with a management plan. During the next few days, I spent long hours with the people I trusted most – both inside and outside the Company – picking their brains, taking their counsel. That next weekend, I happened to be in Seattle for a Washington football game and, on more than a hunch, called my old colleague, Steve Darland. Years earlier, Steve – genetically torn between politics and advertising – had left the advertising business to help run Senator Henry Jackson's fruitless run for the presidency. That quixotic episode over, Darland went back to his day job, settling in as a senior account man at a medium-sized Seattle agency.

He didn't know it at the time, but Steve was Part 3 of the plan I was preparing for Joe and Jack. At dinner after the game, I floated the notion of him re-joining the Thompson Company and working with me in San Francisco as deputy general manager – not in a ceremonial capacity, as he expressly feared, but with broad authority on operational and business issues. "I intend to remain as creative director," I told him, "and I'll need someone to focus on the other areas." This would mean a major life change for Steve, but he was intrigued enough to continue talking and to pay a visit to San Francisco the following week.

Over the course of two days and nights, we took a hard look at the current state of the San Francisco office, at the market in which it was less-than-effectively competing and at Thompson's reputation in the community of clients and new-business prospects. It wasn't a pretty picture. In a misguided effort to be "California cool," JWT had attempted to go toe-to-toe with the likes of Riney, Chiat and Goodby on their terms. They had bought into the myth that "things are different out here"; that, even though the Thompson model had worked enduringly and successfully in every corner of the world, this time and this place called for a new model. In a Faustian bargain, JWT/San Francisco had sold its soul.

Steve and I knew that, try as we might, we never would be a Chiat – nor should we want to be. In a counterintuitive way, we made a calculated judgment that there were a significant number of regional businesses seeking the depth of resources, strategic strength, media power and creative discipline of a very good J. Walter Thompson. This was by no means a sure thing, but we pushed all our chips to the middle of the table and, with a handshake, bet our careers that we could build San Francisco by creating the best J. Walter Thompson office in the U.S. Company.

I flew to New York and presented my plan to Joe and Jack. It consisted of three parts:

1. Jim Agnew would have no presence in San Francisco – no apartment, no office, no client contact and no say-so.

2. In addition to the general manager title, I would retain my role as executive creative director.

3. To partner with me and to assist with the management of the office, I proposed hiring Steve Darland as deputy general manager.

All three parts of the plan met with initial skepticism. It wasn't so much that Jack and Joe bought into the concept of Agnew as "head of the West," but they were worried that he might regard any change in his status as a demotion and place client security in the Los Angeles office at risk. "It's a deal breaker," I said. "I saw what Agnew did to Chuck and he'll try to do the same to me. You don't need that and neither do I."

When they asked if I was biting off too much by remaining as creative director, I assured them I knew how to staff for that. More importantly, I stated the belief that it would be in the best interest of the San Francisco office to be led from the creative point of view.

It was the Darland proposal that generated the greatest

pushback. His absence from the Company for some fifteen years made Steve an outlier in their minds. They suggested, instead, that it would be better for me if they sent someone out from the Chicago or New York offices as deputy. "Darland's my choice," I said, "and I believe the best one. He deserves your considera-tion." And so, by himself – as it had to be – Steve flew east and stepped into the horseshoe with Joe and Jack.

"My meeting with O'Donnell and Peters was tragicomic," Darland said later. "They were unserious, unfocused, never both in Peters' office at the same time, taking calls, stepping out for hall-way meetings. They just wanted to know if I had two heads."

Unfocused or otherwise, Joe called me in San Francisco at meeting's end. "If you're going to run that thing, you should be able to run it the way you want. You've got your deputy."

It's an old truism in the advertising business that an agency's greatest assets go down the elevator at 5:00 every night. If so, we had a severe elevator problem. While, over the course of the previous year, I had been able to kick the creative department into reasonable shape, the account management and ad-services departments were operating in a less than professional – even de-structive – manner. Worse yet, many within these departments still pledged their fealty to Jim Agnew and continued subversive back channel communications with him regarding goings-on in San Francisco.

The problem was most severe among a quartet of account directors, who formed their own clique, played by their own rules, believed that their relationships with clients insulated them from scrutiny, and usually arrived back from lunch after 3:00.

162

It was evident to Steve and me that we had little choice but to cut out the cancer if we expected to build a successful office.

29
The 100th Monkey

In a symbolic act, I chose not to move into the general manager's office, but to remain at my post in the creative department. As with Steve Darland's arrival, it signaled a new way of doing business; where titles and station would be replaced by a dedication to craft. The manager's office was turned into a comfortable place for a quiet meeting. Desks and conference tables were replaced by sofas and easy chairs. As time went on, we took to closing our new-business meetings there, gathering -- just a few of us -- to take questions and ask for the sale. Shelves along two long walls were stocked with books relating to advertising, the communications industry, sociology and the culture of a wider world. Visitors and staff were encouraged to take any book of interest and leave another for the edification of others. We ordered a hundred copies of James Webb Young's primer on "A Technique for Producing Ideas," a volume that conjured the heritage and influence of the Thompson Company.

Just as the Executive Dining Room at JWT/New York assumed a different guise after 5:00 – as a bar called The Meeting Club – so the San Francisco manager's office became an after hours lounge called The 100th Monkey. The name derived from a contemporary book about social change that involved the 30-year study of a colony of monkeys on the island of Koshima. Scientists observed that ideological breakthrough involving cultural behavior happened when that behavior reached a certain critical mass – for argument's sake, when the adopters increased from 99 to 100 monkeys. More remarkably, once critical mass had been achieved, the new behavior appeared on other islands --as if plucked out of thin air, communicated mind to mind. We took it upon ourselves to go about creating critical mass for our clients. In San Francisco, we would be agents of change.

The Meeting Club had bartenders in tuxedoes and so did The 100th Monkey. Dues were calculated in such a way that the highest-paid of us would contribute the most, and others would pay less and less according to the size of their salary. Secretaries could join for $15.00, which entitled them to beer and wine for a year as well as drinks for the occasional guest. The 100th Monkey proved to be a great barrier breaker. It was a way to keep people at work longer, talking about the business of the day with colleagues from throughout the agency. Conversation sparked ideas which spilled over into offices as account, strategic planning and creative teams worked into the night trying to come up with a new Chevron position or outflank each other for the next Sprint spot.

In this market of hot, young creative shops, Steve and I felt it was important to remind and to educate the people in the office – as well as the client community at large – about the tremendous history, global resources and profound influence of JWT. That in mind, we carried on another long-standing New York tradition:

"Thompson Nights." As invitation-only evening events, we presented programs of contemporary interest to high-level clients, new-business prospects and members of the advertising press, followed by an open reception and, then, an intimate dinner. Speakers included the likes of Milton Friedman, Pierre Salinger, William Randolph Hearst, Jr. and, in a lighter vein, Joe Montana and Ray Bradbury.

As we endeavored to create a culture of "us" in the agency, collectively building the kind of place where dedicated and talented people would strive to do good work together, we first had to break down the office's existing and morale-destructive cliques. Chief among them was the group of entrenched senior account people who resented the intrusion of new management on their territory and continued to feed Agnew information he had no business knowing.

As fate would have it, an unfortunate drop in revenue from the previous account losses of Activision and ComputerLand allowed us to justify a general reduction in force throughout the agency. Out went Mike Barton, the Diet Center account director, who was generally half in the bag by 10:00 in the morning and, because of that, had been invited never to show up at their corporate headquarters again. Out went Dick Rader, a major conniver, who had long outlived his usefulness. Out went Kathy Hoskins, the mean-spirited head of broadcast production, who, after a morning of browbeating the creatives, generally joined the account directors for their booze-fueled lunches. (Like Mac Churchill, Kathy made a particularly memorable final gesture. At the meeting with me and our human resources director informing her that she was to be let go, Kathy walked over to my desk and spat in my face.)

A new attitude began to emerge and it didn't take long for the word to get out. We made it a point to cultivate headhunters, art reps and the otherwise talkative to help us communicate that new leadership and a new vitality had arrived at JWT. Internally, we redoubled our efforts to teach and practice The Thompson Way, training those in account management, planning, creative and media in the art of developing focused strategies, writing creative briefs and unearthing big ideas – no matter from which discipline they came.

Dividends began to pay almost immediately. In late 1986, we were invited to pitch for Stewart Anderson's Black Angus Restaurants, a chain of high-end steak houses that extended up and down the Pacific Coast. Black Angus had most recently been at Riney and our major competition for this go-around was reported to be the equally hot Goodby Berlin & Silverstein. We heard through the grapevine that the client had wondered out loud if an agency the size of Thompson could deliver the kind of quick response creative solutions their category demanded. We intended to blast that misconception out of the water with a daring demonstration.

A week before the presentation, we called Julia Stewart, Black Angus' VP of marketing and threw down a gauntlet. We invited her to bring us a particularly vexing problem the restaurants were currently facing and to brief us as the meeting began. We promised to deliver a solution by day's end.

"… new gm Bill Lane's emerging young management team gave the client an informal, hands on 'day at J. Walter Thompson,' climaxed by a show of fire drill advertising," wrote Jon Berry of *AdWeek*.

Indeed we did. A special project team of art directors, copywriters, and account and media planners left the conference room after the briefing and under the gun while Steve and I and the other department heads carried on with the heart of our presentation. In little more than four hours, the team returned with a clever strategy – brought to life by videotaped man-on- the-street interviews – a completely scripted radio campaign, and a detailed media plan. Point-of-sale materials were designed and executed – right down to table tents.

By the time we delivered our close in the comfort of The 100th Monkey, the decision was a fait accompli. "They just bowled us over," Stewart told Berry. "They were innovative and enthusiastic. They were not the Thompson many people think of." We were awarded the account on the spot. (A brief dust up occurred a few days later when *Ad Week* asked Andy Berlin of Goodby Berlin why he thought they had lost the competition. "I guess the client didn't want breakthrough creative," he said. "They just wanted someone safe." When asked to comment I took the bait. "No, the reason they came to J. Walter Thompson was they were tired of the shoot-from-the-hip solutions they've been getting from the likes of Goodby." When told of my response, Andy phone-tracked me to Scott's restaurant in the Embarcadero -- where I was having lunch with New York headhunter Judy Wald -- and personally threatened me with bodily harm.)

As Steve focused on client service and operations, I continued to concentrate on building the creative department and improving the work. Jon Hyde, an art director by trade and a Thompson man by history, re-joined the company to serve as associate creative director. Jon had a fine eye, an adult wardrobe and provided a sober counterbalance to the prevailing insanity. As in Detroit, I had managed to gather a representative sample of the town's creative rebels and rapscallions. A bit disingenuously, I held them to only two rules: (1) treat client business very, very seriously and (2) do great work. The little darlings repaid my trust by discovering a hole-in-the-wall bar on Martin Street where they would repair in the early mornings for stout Bloody Marys before showing up at the office.

Where we really needed a radical infusion of new blood -- and why I had been talking with Judy Wald -- was in television production. Change had to begin at the top, where executive producer Bob LaChance had allowed standards to fall, quality to drop and the agency's reputation in the Hollywood community to suffer. Claiming age discrimination, LaChance sued the agency – and me personally -- on his way out the door. The case went to trial, and a dozen witnesses -- most of whom were from the old regime, the ones who I had recently fired -- testified against me. Their claims were blasphemous, their language scurrilous, and their veracity apparently unbelievable. The jury ruled unanimously in our favor.

Our brightest young producer, Craig Allen, chafing under the leadership of the blasé LaChance and the demanding Hoskins had left for another agency. Jim Phox was employed merely to do Chevron's bidding. The cupboard was bare.

We had little recourse but to scour the country for just the right person to rebuild the department; someone with the box office credentials that would lend us instant credibility. And so began the curious case of Mickey Paradise.

Mickey had spent his professional life at some of Chicago's finest agencies and his reel consisted of award-winning commercials from beginning to end. His resume showed that he had jumped from agency to agency more than most, but our contacts in the California commercial production community had nothing but good things to say about him.

On first meeting, Mickey made an indelible impression. Standing no taller than 5'4 – and with a full beard – he bore a remarkable resemblance to Henry de Toulouse-Lautrec. His conversation tended toward the "Have you stopped beating your wife?" kind of questions, especially when it came time to challenge his eye-popping expenses. "It's the way things are done at the great agencies," he'd say. "You want to be great, don't you?")

Yes, we wanted to be great and Mickey, for the moment, gained us enure to the best directors in Hollywood. Suddenly, the likes of Leslie Dektor, Graham Henman and Joe Sedelmaier were taking our calls and doing our projects. After a six-month flourish, about the only one not taking our calls was Mickey Paradise himself. He had kept a residence in Chicago and commuted back and forth to visit his children, so it wasn't unusual for him to be out of the office frequently. But, little by little and more and more, Mickey became permanently elsewhere. I tried to locate him just to have a talk. I couldn't. I called around to his pals in Hollywood and asked them to have him call me. He didn't. Finally, I had no choice but to fire the missing Mickey Paradise.

And I would have done it, too. If I'd been able to find him.

If one is fortunate, as was I, there comes a moment in a long career when "they" become "us." And so it happened that, in the fall of 1986, I was invited to J. Walter Thompson headquarters at 466 Lexington Avenue for a rite of corporate passage. Much as I had almost 20 years earlier – on my very first day with the Company – I waited in a freshly pressed suit and just-shined shoes in an executive floor lobby. Gathered behind closed doors was a small group of JWT's most senior professionals from Europe, Asia, Latin America and the U.S. When, after a few pregnant moments, the door opened, I was invited inside as a duly elected member of Thompson's worldwide board of directors.

If not awestruck, I was decidedly deferential to these men of station I had long admired. Among the more colorful (and profane) was Lee Preschel, the venerable area director of Latin America. For more than a decade, Lee had artfully managed 18 offices stretching from Mexico to Argentina, many on the raw edges of civilization. (There's a rumor – which Preschel doesn't deny – that, as he moved from country to country, he often carried a concealed handgun.)

Michael Cooper-Evans from London had turned to advertising to save his neck. As a young man, he had been a none-too-successful Formula One racecar driver, known more for his spectacular crashes than his triumphant finishes. He confessed to having broken almost every bone in his body, which he said well qualified him for client contact. Jeremy Bullmore, chairman of London and a gentler man, had earned his early reputation as one of England's most distinguished copywriters. Indeed, upon retirement, he continued on as Britain's pre-eminent man of advertising letters. ("Jeremy Bullmore remains the one person in British advertising for whom the brilliance to bullshit ratio is 100:0," wrote Nigel Bogle of Bartle Bogle Hegarty.)

Even though a healthy amount of parliamentary procedure went on at JWT board meetings, it wasn't Roberts Rules of Order that gave them their true texture and abiding value. Collegiality happened after hours in quiet bars over dark whiskey. Friendships were forged, advice was dispensed and bridges were built that made a far-flung company seem more like one.

Under Joe O'Donnell's gavel, it was the job of this board to keep the professional flame of the Thompson Company burning brightly. Unlike most of its major competitors, who had formed their philosophies and achieved their success primarily from a single office, JWT had instead grown its brand in the disparate soils of a wider world. It opened a London office in 1899, and by the late 1920s had offices in more than 30 countries. While sharing common business practices and operational standards, these JWT offices tended to act more as a federation, reflecting the advertising character of the cultures in which they competed.

All that began to change with the rise in importance of what are now known as the "multi-nationals." As Thompson clients Ford, Nestle, Unilever, Kraft and Kodak expanded their markets worldwide, they created a need for a global advertising agency that would operate country-to-country and office-to-office in strategic and creative lock step. If a client attended a planning meeting in Frankfurt, it should feel the same as if he were sitting down with his account team in Buenos Aires.

It's from these seeds that The Thompson Way sprang; where the "T- Plan" became standard operating procedure; where the rigors of review boards helped sustain a uniform level of quality; where "stimulus and response" became a creative mantra. By the time I joined the board, these principles were ingrained and championed by a new generation of members – my own – including Miles Colebrick of London, Ron Burns of Canada and Steve Bowen and Jim Patterson of New York. (Patterson – for those who have not been on an airplane or to a beach in the last fifteen years – is now James Patterson, the best selling author in the whole wide world. Before he abandoned writing Burger King commercials and began spinning tales of mystery and intrigue, he was just plain Jim.)

All this was very nice, but, after all, I still had important work back home. Fortunately, now staffed and operating as a unified, motivated unit, San Francisco was continuing its run of new business successes. American Hawaii Cruise Lines followed close on the heels of Black Angus. A real coup was the hard-fought win of Jenny Craig Weight Loss Centers, an account that relied on large doses of aggressive advertising and grew to be San Francisco's second largest in billing.

But, behemoth Sprint, with its voracious appetite for new ideas and fresh work, continued to occupy most of our time. The paint would barely be dry on one set of new commercials, when Big Ed Carter would be in our creative kitchen trying to cook up new ones. It's difficult to classify anything in this relationship as "out of the ordinary," because hardly anything about it was "in the ordinary." Strategy sessions would be held in restaurants wherever Ed happened to be traveling that week. He didn't value formal meetings with fancy charts so much as he did random thoughts scribbled on the backs of cocktail napkins. Presentations would take place under the most slapstick of circumstances. If you'd walked into the JWT conference room one evening in the fall of 1986, you would have seen me standing precariously on a chair, holding a storyboard above Carter – who was lying supine on the floor due to an attack of lumbago. In pain or not, he was gesticulating wildly like a big bug that had flipped over on its back.

The campaign in question had been developed by Rik Gloff as an idea called "Clear Across America," designed to visually track Sprint's progress in building the first and only fiber optic network, well, clear across America. Ed had taken the 100% fiber optic bit in his teeth and was running with it faster than his legal department – or ours – would allow. "God damn lawyers," he'd scream. "Why do we have to keep tellin' folks it ain't done yet?"

As we had counseled Sprint from the beginning, the promise of fiber optics – the progress, if you will – was news enough to sustain interest. But that wasn't good enough or fast enough for Big Ed Carter. No, we were at war and he wanted to slam AT&T at every turn. Our fiber was underground and they still had all those telephone poles and microwave towers. So, at his direction, we developed – and actually shot – a commercial where we blew up a tower in Chanute, Kansas.

Amid this chaos, a major marketing idea managed to come shining through – a glistening little customer-acquisition lure called the "FON Card." In a moment of creative insight, we'd hit upon the notion that FON was – at the same time – a neat acronym for Fiber Optic Network, and a unique homophone for PHONE. As a sampling device, the FON Card had few equals. If you followed the dialing instructions on the back, you could gain access to US Sprint – and, hopefully to fiber optics – from any telephone, no matter who your regular carrier was.

The card was designed out of a silvery material called Mylar that made it look very 21st century. And, in a stroke of media genius, we chose to distribute it, not by mailing it out, but by tipping it into airline in-flight magazines – perforated six to a page. FON Cards became a minor rage, literally flying out of the magazines and into travelers' wallets. In a very short time, we had enticed tens of thousands of prospects into sampling the Sprint difference. (As an indication of FON Card demand, there was a moment when every Mylar supplier in the United States ran out of inventory.)

As usual, Ed pushed even further. Not only did he urge us to come up with all sorts of additional services the FON Card might provide – none of which were ever implemented – he invited us to make a major presentation to Sprint management urging them to change the name of the whole corporation to "The FON Company."

In theory, that might not have been a bad idea. But in one of those quirky conversations that only occur in advertising meetings or Peter Sellers movies, there was a serious debate on just how people would pronounce "FON." One particularly dim executive suggested that we ran the danger of becoming known as the "Fawn" company. That mangled thought managed to slow the train just enough to table the FON Company discussion forever.

Meanwhile, Jim Sanderson was noodling around with an idea for the ultimate anti-AT&T campaign. It would send Big Ed into paroxysms of joy. It would generate test scores higher than any Sprint campaign ever. And it would almost get us fired.

31
Coup d'Etat

On the morning of January 21, 1987, it began to snow a deep snow in New York City. Trying to hold an umbrella against the wind, I made my way up Lexington Avenue from the Grand Hyatt Hotel to a conference room at JWT, where I was to meet Ed Carter and his young acolyte Chris Clouser. A new Sprint advertising campaign was about to break and Ed was eager to give the press a preview. I'd opened the meeting by showing the new commercials and Ed proceeded to field questions, voice rising as always, arms flailing as usual. I felt a tap on my shoulder. It was Loraine Rosen, Joe O'Donnell's secretary.

"Joe wants to see you," she said.

I followed Thompson etiquette – which always places client business above agency matters – and remained with Ed and

Chris, intending to see Joe when the press conference ended.

"I said Joe wants to see you." It was Loraine again, uncharacteristically insistent.

Slightly embarrassed, I excused myself from the meeting with the promise to return in a few moments. I took the elevator down to the 3rd floor and walked to Joe's corner office. He shut the door behind us.

"I'm moving against Johnston," he said. "We've discovered some serious irregularities overseas and we believe the Company could take a big reputation hit if we don't act now. I'm going to present a letter to the outside board members on Friday, which a number of us have signed. I'd like you to sign it, too." The letter described "a very disturbing management pattern where ethical shortcuts are condoned and if found out, are covered up." It suggested that Don be removed as chairman of JWT Group. And, while it wasn't written down that Joe be installed as his successor, that logical conclusion was evident between the lines. In addition to O'Donnell, the letter was signed by Lee Preschel, Jack Peters, Burt Metter and Victor Gutierrez, JWT's chief financial officer.

"Joe," I said. "I have no first-hand knowledge of any of this. And I don't see how this action will do my office, my people or my clients any good. I need time to think."

"Suit yourself. Go ahead and think it over. You've got 'til the end of the day."

I'd barely escaped Joe's office when Jack Peters grabbed me. "Get in here, kid," he said. Jack closed his door, too. "Did you sign the letter?" His voice was urgent. "You really need to sign that letter." As I began my spiel to buy time, Jack's phone rang and, while he was distracted, I made an escape.

(It would be the last time I saw Jack. A couple of years later, a deranged young man – a family friend who had attended high school with Jack's sons – attacked him in the swimming pool of his Greenwich, Connecticut home. With a 9mm pistol, he pumped a bullet into Jack's head and another into his heart.)

I didn't dare return to the Sprint meeting, but instead fled to the Grand Hyatt. By this time, the snow was flying horizontally and had turned the sidewalks into skating rinks. Even my room was no refuge. The message light was blinking, blinking, blinking. Joe had called once, Jack twice. I phoned my friend, music man Paul Hoffman. "Bo," I said. "Can I sleep on your couch tonight?" I showed up at his studio on West 23rd with a toothbrush and a decision to make.

I couldn't help but wonder what had precipitated Joe's move. He was in line to take over the entire JWT Group in two years anyway, so why act now? And while Don Johnston's performance as head of the Group had not been above criticism – especially from Wall Street – disappointing financial results had been its nature, never malfeasance. An analyst from Dean Witter summed things up: "The general impression is that Johnston has done a good job of running the agency as an agency," he said. "but that he simply has not paid enough attention to the bottom line." As far as I knew, Don's integrity was above reproach. My decision slowly came clear. I had followed Joe to Detroit. I had followed him up the corporate ladder to the board. But I couldn't follow him now.

As the snow-blown afternoon turned into a wickedly cold

evening, events continued to drift toward the surreal. About 9 o'clock, Paul and I fought our way through the bitter wind to Sugar Reef, a favorite Caribbean restaurant where, even on a stormy night, it took a twenty-dollar bill to get a table. As the rum flowed, we became aware of a disturbance near the entrance to the restaurant. A homeless man had made his way inside, wedged himself in the foyer and refused to leave. When the owner couldn't budge the man by himself, burly Paul helped him execute an emphatic heave ho.

Peace was restored – but not for long. I looked up to see the recently expelled man, a knife in hand, rushing wildly at Paul, who was sitting with his back to the door. A shouted warning, a waiter's tackle, and a sudden tuck prevented Paul from being stabbed between the shoulder blades.

I deliberately stayed away from the Grand Hyatt until the middle of Saturday night. At about 4:00 in the morning, I returned to gather my things. Not only was the message light blinking, but also several hand-written messages had been slipped under the door. Joe, Jack, Jack, Joe, Joe, Jack. The last one had been dated Friday morning. I caught a cab to JFK and headed home to San Francisco on a mid-Sunday morning flight. I got the news when I landed: O'Donnell had been fired and led from the building by armed security officers. I was to call Don Johnston immediately.

As I dialed Don, I thanked God I hadn't signed that bloody letter, especially when I learned that Lee Preschel, Bert Metter and Jack Peters had also been fired.

"Hello, Don. It's Bill Lane." Don and I had always enjoyed the warmest of relationships, so I was a bit taken aback by the coldness in his voice.

"Are you with me or against me?" That's all he said.

When I assured him that my loyalty was without question, he said: "Very well. Be at a board meeting in New York tomorrow morning at 9."

So, I unpacked my bag only to pack it again for another trip east. As I was about to head for the airport, I received a call from Jim Agnew.

"Are you okay?" he asked.

"I guess so. I just got off the phone with Don and I'm leaving in a minute for a board meeting in New York. Why do you ask?"

"Well, when you disappeared for a couple of days, they hired private detectives to find you. They staked out your hotel and checked flights to the West Coast. Your office didn't even know where you were." (Actually, my private secretary Deb Groth knew exactly where I was every moment. But you couldn't get information out of the fiercely loyal Deb with Korean water torture.) It was obvious they didn't have Sam Spade on the case. Holing up at Paul's was, for me, like hiding in plain sight.

That Monday morning board meeting can only be described as Kafka-esque. In place of the old bonhomie, there was an unusual formality and chill. Don took the floor and held it for an hour. He told us of O'Donnell's charges and that it was at his insistence that Joe present them to the outside board members to resolve things once and for all. When O'Donnell was given that opportunity, board member David L. Yunich, retired vice-chairman of Macy's, was quoted as saying "his speech was incoherent, unprofessional, and highly emotional, to the point that it was upsetting to everyone."

At the conclusion of the meeting, Johnston pulled me aside and asked for my resignation from the board. "I'm going to need to operate with a smaller group," he explained. It gets very slippery the closer you get to the top.

32
Two if by Sea

The wag who said that there's no such thing as bad publicity never had to run an advertising agency during stormy weather. As soon as word got out about Joe O'Donnell's perfidy, there was blood in San Francisco's waters. As a rule, big clients don't like their agencies in the news and J. Walter Thompson was front-page stuff in both the *Chronicle* and the *Examiner,* not to mention *The New York Times* and *Wall Street Journal.* I called a management committee meeting to discuss the attempted coup, especially as it might affect client security. Steve and I then set about talking to our clients directly.

"Shit, I don't care," was Ed Carter's response on hearing that O'Donnell had been fired. On thinking back to the incident when Joe had chided Sprint for beginning the briefing meeting without him, he added: "I always thought he was a horse's ass anyhow."

The Chevron Corporation was quite another matter. We'd been involved in a delicate situation with them ever since 1984 when they acquired the Gulf Oil Company. In an effort to seamlessly blend the marketing operations of the two organizations,

Chevron appointed Jim Gordon, Gulf's advertising manager, to succeed Herb Hammerman.

While Hammerman was an odd duck, at least he had been our odd duck. Unfortunately, Jim Gordon was Y&R's odd duck. Not too long after he had transferred to San Francisco, Gordon approached me with a Hobson's choice. It seems that at Gulf, he'd become quite close to the Houston-based Y&R account director. Would I consider, he asked, hiring his friend to take over the Chevron account at J. Walter Thompson?

"But Jim," I said, "that means you want me to fire our account director who's been a part of the Chevron team for ten years."

"I'm not telling you what to do," he said. "Just asking. Just asking."

Over dinner a few nights later, I was telling Ed Carter about Gordon's request. "Are you gonna do it?" he asked.

"Nope. I'm not going to let this new guy tell me how to run my agency."

"You're a damn fool, Lane." He quoted Lyndon Johnson: "It's better to have your enemies inside the tent pissing out than outside the tent pissing in."

And a damn fool I turned out to be. A month or so later, Y&R transferred Jim Gordon's account director from Houston to San Francisco, and a few months after that, Chevron announced that they would hold an agency competition for "new thinking" on their retail business. It wasn't earth-shaking news that the other agency was Y&R.

For some time, we suspected that Y&R had been feeding Chevron daily reports on the attempted hostile takeover of JWT by a British company called WPP and its leader Martin Sorrell, who, though a small fish as corporate raiders go, had the appetite of a Great White. (WPP stood for "Wire and Plastic Products," founded ingloriously in 1971 as a manufacturer of grocery shopping baskets. The name recalls the mythical World Wide Wickets, hilariously portrayed in the Broadway musical *How to Succeed in Business Without Really Trying*. That was done for laughs. But, as history would prove, lord help the sap who laughed at Martin Sorrell and WPP.)

Agencies had long been thought to be immune to such piracy. After all, practically their entire bankable inventory was people and clients, who – the prevailing wisdom went – would simply up and leave at the whiff of takeover. Indeed, the word got back to us that Chevron would be none too pleased if their agency fell into foreign hands.

But a weak bottom line and O'Donnell's coup attempt had suddenly put advertising's greatest brand "in play." JWT had history and reputation; Martin Sorrell had cash. Johnston fought hard. When asked at an analysts meeting how he would act to a hostile takeover bid, he replied "Equally hostile."

In the middle of all this, I asked him to take part in our Chevron presentation. He'd been key to San Francisco winning the Chevron account in the first place and, over the years, had maintained a close relationship with Ken Derr, Chevron's president. But, when I called New York with the date, I was told Don would be in Mexico. If we wanted him in San Francisco for the meeting, we'd have to charter a private jet.

And so we did. The presentation was brimming with "new

ideas." Johnston's part was dramatic and – we thought – persuasive. But, as we awaited the outcome of the competition, events began to overtake us. On June 10th, Sorrell made a handsome unsolicited offer for J. Walter Thompson. A half a billion dollars later, we no longer controlled our own destiny. In a battle between Wall Street and Madison Avenue, Wall Street had won.

A few days later, Chevron Retail followed Johnston out the door.

As a fitting bit of punctuation on the whole exercise, Dan Christ, our chief financial officer, walked an invoice into my office in late July. "Did you authorize this?" he asked. I had. It was the bill for Johnston's jet: $26,000.

Sorrell's first action as owner was a clever one: he hired back Burt Manning and made him CEO, a stroke that served to calm the troops and soothe our clients. Burt took quick command, calling a board meeting in New York. When it convened, I was proposed for election a second time. As I waited outside the board chamber for what seemed an inordinately long time, a debate raged within. Jim Patterson – for reasons he has kept to himself – opposed my election. All this was unknown to me as I was finally admitted to be sworn in, though I could sense an undercurrent of tension among the members. During the day's proceedings, I remained quiet – uncharacteristically so, I'm told. When Burt asked for a motion to adjourn, Cooper-Evans demurred and, in that clipped British way of his said: "We can't adjourn, yet. Lane hasn't said one shit-ty thing all day." Laughter lightened the mood if not mended the wound.

While this drama was playing out, Jim Sanderson and the Sprint team went about developing what everyone believed was the campaign that would put AT&T in its place, once and for all. If Big Ed Carter and the Kansas City group had still been firmly in charge, it might indeed have done that. Alas, corporate owner GTE was becoming more and more involved by the day and made it clear that all major advertising decisions would have to go through their approval process. As an agency, we had never met with GTE higher-ups (we were told it would be impolitic), and that lack of familiarity nearly proved our undoing.

Sanderson's creative notion was brilliant: while Sprint's management was agile, friendly and customer responsive, AT&T's management was smug, slow and could give a damn about the lowly customer. They were so many "Fat Cats." And that's just the way we showed them. As originally conceived, the commercials starred a real, live tubby feline. In blasé voiceover, he spoke in an accent that sounded like a cross between Bette Davis and William F. Buckley. Our Fat Cat was always riding first class -- never in coach with the hoi polloi. He traveled by limousine and wallowed in cash from the exorbitant fees he charged customers. He worked for a company called FAT&T. FAT&T management regularly met in a cavernous boardroom, all mahogany and leather. Stern-faced portraits of presidents past glowered down from ornate, gold-leaf frames. (Keep that picture in mind.)

Sprint's Kansas City management was so excited about the campaign and confident of its ultimate approval by GTE, that they authorized the agency to begin pre-production. As that process developed, director Stu Hagmann came up with the idea of casting a real person as the Fat Cat and dressing him in the appropriate fur and tail. Comedian Avery Schreiber was to play the starring role.

184

For such a payday, he even agreed to shave his trademark moustache. It was all very funny – until the day of the presentation.

GTE headquarters were located in Stamford, Connecticut, just over the border from New York. (Actually, they had been located in Manhattan until 1970, when an anti-war group in a bad mood blew up their building.) Steve Sanchez, Sanderson and I flew in from San Francisco. We were joined by Burt Manning – which was appropriate – since Jim Brophy, GTE's president, would chair their side.

As we walked into the presentation area, Sanderson shot me a sidelong glance. It was a cavernous boardroom, all mahogany and leather. Stern-faced portraits of past presidents glowered down from ornate, gold-leaf frames. It looked exactly like our first storyboard – one with FAT&T management fairly exulting in their disdain for customers. Yikes.

James Brophy was not the jolliest of men to begin with and his normally grim visage grew grimmer as Sanderson went through first commercial. His associates – arrayed to the right and left of him – looked remarkably like those we had drawn, Fat Cats all. As Sanderson finished, he was met with stone-cold silence. It didn't last long.

"This is the most disgusting advertising I have ever seen," Brophy began. "It's tasteless, offensive – and we won't have our name on it!"

Manning handed me a note under the table. "You say something," it said. "Give me a minute to think."

I don't remember what I said, but, to his credit (and my eternal admiration), Manning rose to our defense. "Jim, Jim," he said calmly to Brophy. "I'm surprised at your response. Whether you like it or not, this is what people think of big telephone companies like AT&T. It's important to show them that you're not like that – Sprint isn't like that." Manning went on a bit longer and the presentation continued until its end. Of course, Fat Cat never ran. But Manning got us out of the room.

"That's going to cost us $50,000." Executive producer Craig Allen was in my office. Apparently, we had signed some sort of agreement with Avery Schreiber that, if he shaved off his moustache, and if for some reason the campaign never ran, we'd have to pay him fifty grand.

It was an expensive month.

33
L'Affaire O.J.

The constant and unholy pursuit of new business occasionally spills into strange waters. In the summer of 1987, director Fred Levinson invited me to Los Angeles to meet a friend of his. "He's got a TV show idea," Fred said. "He needs some creative help and I told him about you. I think his show would be great for some of your clients." The vision of dollar signs danced in my head.

His friend happened to be 6'2" and weight 212 pounds and have a Heisman Trophy in his living room. Orenthal James Simpson met us at the door of his Rockingham Drive home as if we were long, lost brothers. As we shook hands, mine disappeared into his. Rockingham was a sprawling sun-splashed ranch-style house with a pool and a tennis court out back and a parade of friends, family and hangers-on shuffling in and out at all hours.

We sat at a large refectory table in the kitchen where O.J. had spread out the evidence of his idea. "It's a cartoon show with characters who are famous athletes in real life," he began. "We're 'America's First Team' and we have superpowers to do great deeds and help kids who get in trouble. Iron Mike is Mike Tyson – and he can lift up a locomotive with his bare hands. Pistol Pete Rose is faster than a speeding bullet and Larry Bird can jump higher than a building. Chrissie Evert has x-ray vision to see through anything. And O.J? He can fly. The real athletes are going to do the voices."

I studied several preliminary sketches of "America's First Team" dressed in superpower tights and capes. Irony fairly dripped..

As we talked, O.J.'s wife Nicole breezed by on her way out the door to run errands. "Hey, baby, meet Bill. He's gonna help us with the show." Nicole was California blonde, tan, and too beautiful. She paused just long enough to say "hi" and was gone.

O.J's idea wasn't half bad. And, while it wasn't right for any of San Francisco's current clients, it might prove an attractive lure for prospective ones. From a Company-wide standpoint, it seemed a perfect fit for Chicago's Kellogg's and Kraft or for New York's Toys R Us.

I suggested we bring in Rik Gloff -- who had experience in writing for episodic TV -- to help develop scripts. And so began a several months' odyssey that wove its way clear to Burt Manning's office.

A generation before Tiger Woods, O.J. Simpson was America's first true crossover star -- equally beloved by blacks and whites, attractive to women, admired by men. He had a magnetism that drew everyone to him and a manner that made the world want to be his friend. I attended a World Series Game at Yankee stadium in 1978 – at the height of O.J.'s celebrity – when the crowd rose as one in a thunderous cheer for a reason that had nothing to do with the game. O.J. Simpson had entered the field level box area and was making his way to his seat. The game paused. Reggie Jackson turned and gave O.J. a wave.

Advertisers flocked to O.J. for endorsements. Indeed, Fred Levinson had met him while shooting a famous series of spots for Hertz ("Go, O.J., go!") and the two had become close friends. (Nicole's sister Denise held her wedding reception poolside in Fred's Beverly Hills backyard.) Over the summer and into the fall, Gloff and I would fly to L.A. every other week or so to review message themes, story ideas and incidental characters. (One character was not so incidental. As a sort of narrative glue, Gloff invented "Stats," a computerized droid, who could spit out earned run averages and slugging percentages at the drop of a trivia question. Howard Cosell had agreed to supply the voice.)

O.J. and Fred pitched the show to all three networks and their response was encouraging. The general feeling was that we stood a much better shot at scoring a Saturday morning time slot if we could deliver a key advertiser. That understood, I began to develop a presentation to advertisers involving audience data, buying habits and promotional opportunities. We wouldn't limit our outreach to J. Walter Thompson clients, but it was understood that we would give them the first shot.

I was gradually drawn into the O.J. orbit and had the opportunity to watch this cultural phenomenon at close range. Like many celebrities, O.J. was needy. He clearly fed off of the adulation of others, and they were all too willing to subjugate their own good sense if it allowed them to hang around the great man. How else do you explain the weekly Wednesday night poker games at Rockingham? These evenings ran heavy with expensive scotch, contraband Cuban cigars and high stakes. (Once again I was a dollar slot player in a sea of major money. I declined to play but was invited to attend anyway.) O.J. drew the players from a pool of country club cowboys and wealthy Beverly Hills merchants. Each tried to outdo the other in locker-room bravado and street-wise language. (One evening, O.J. pal and Oakland Raider running back Marcus Allen stopped by to say "hi" on his way to the movies. His date was Eleanor Mondale, former Vice President Walter Mondale's daughter.

"What the hell is Marcus doing with Eleanor Mondale?" someone asked after they'd gone.

O.J. took a puff from his Cuban. "Fuckin' her, I guess." Raucous laughter.)

During the course of a Wednesday game, thousands of dollars would be won and lost. Usually one or more of the high rollers went home lighter in the five figures. O.J. never lost. He openly cheated. Everybody knew. Nobody cared. After all, they could tell their friends they'd lost a bundle to The Juice.

Presentation in order, O.J., Fred and I hit the road to pitch "America's First Team" to advertisers. We found that getting meetings was easy. The lure of sitting with the great O.J. Simpson opened a lot of doors and assured the attendance of executives more senior than they needed to be at this stage of the project. Our first few presentations were in Chicago, and, while we had no firm commitments, the reception to the show concept had been positive.

It was in high spirits that we hit New York. As a first stop, I had scheduled a sit-down with Burt Manning. His endorsement would certainly carry weight with JWT's clients. Now, this was an out-of-body experience. As usual, I let O.J. do most of the talking. Watching him and the usually reserved Manning interact was marvelous theater. We left 466 Lexington with hearty handshakes, lusty back slaps and high hopes. "America's First Team" was on its way.

But enterprises such as television shows take their sweet time from concept to production. And, thinking back, perhaps our so-called "positive" meetings were not so much honest consideration of the project as they were excuses for hero worshipers to meet The Juice. Anyway, one by one, the wheels of the concept began to fall off and client interest cooled. It didn't help that Mike Tyson chose that season to degenerate into a woman-beating menace. Or that Pete Rose was caught betting on baseball and was banned from the game for life. Not to mention that, a year or two down the road, something went awfully wrong up the road from Rockingham.

All the while this dalliance with Hollywood was playing out, my future was being kicked around from Kansas City to New York and, curiously, to the District of Columbia. As in 1968, I was about to be drafted – although this time, my greetings came not from Richard M. Nixon, but from one Christopher E. Clouser.

Part IV

34
The Cult of Clouser

People tended to take an immediate liking to Chris Clouser. He had a certain charismatic charm, knew his way around office and other politics and played nice with elders. He was the classic embodiment of "fair-haired boy." Or Sammy Glick.

Chris showed up on San Francisco's doorstep as Ed Carter's batman, fresh out of Sprint's P.R. department, new to this advertising business. But he was eager to learn, seemed to enjoy the flash and dash of it, and satisfied Ed's desire to spread the Gospel of Sprint through the press. We began to travel together as a presentation tag team. Chris would woo them; I would wow them. We fell into friendship – but evidently not yet the kind that yielded secrets.

So, I was surprised when Burt Manning called with news. As I recall, his narrative went about like this: "Just heard from Chris Clouser. Chris has been named director of advertising and marketing at Bell Atlantic. It's a $75 million account and he'll give it to us without a competition if we move you back to New York to run it."

Whew. I could have refused, I suppose, and kept on as general manager and creative director of what had become one of San Francisco's most dynamic and successful agencies. I could have remained in my wonderful house in Marin County and driven every morning across the Golden Gate Bridge to the most elegant city in America. But that would have run against the "Thompson Code," not written down anyplace, but as solid and inviolate as Gibraltar itself. Personal life always took a back seat. Help get the Company ready for a new business presentation in California while your wife is having a baby in Connecticut? Ace staff man Roy Glah did that. Return to Detroit in the middle of a vacation on England's Cornwall Coast for a last-minute meeting on Ford? I did that. ("What the hell are you doing here?" a surprised Doug McClure asked when he saw me. "This wasn't important enough to ruin a vacation.") When Burt Manning told me about Chris and Bell Atlantic, my answer was assumed before the question was asked. Of course I would move. Duty always called.

Having Steve Darland in place made my transition to New York easier, and, in some ways inevitable. In our years together, Steve had demonstrated superior organizational and leadership skills and was more than ready to step into the top spot. Indeed, during his tenure as San Francisco manager, office billings increased almost threefold, every client continuing to pay a full 15%.

And so my long journey with Chris Clouser began. Clouser's career had followed an unusual course. While many of our generation dabbled in politics in the late 60s and early 70s, Chris made it full time job. He joined the staff of Missouri Senator Thomas Eagleton and got a taste of the seductive – and sometimes destructive – power of Washington. Eagleton's star enjoyed a brief ascendancy when he was nominated to run for Vice-President on Eugene McCarthy's 1972 ticket. But, during the campaign, it was revealed that Eagleton had had mental health issues, had undergone electroshock therapy, and was currently on Thorazine, an anti-psychotic drug for treating the suicidal. This scared the bejeepers out of the McCarthy folks. Eagleton was forced to beat an ignominious retreat from the hustings and, barely two months before the election, he resigned from the ticket.

Understandably shaken by the events, Kansas City Chris did a logical thing: he returned home to join the communications department of Hallmark, the town's signature corporation. In those days, Hallmark was noted for producing distinguished programming for network television (*The Hallmark Hall of Fame*) and the intoxicating allure of big-time entertainment events was visited upon Clouser. It stayed with him throughout the many stops of his career, none of which he stayed at very long, most of which I attended.

He arrived at Sprint with slicked back hair and stars in his eyes. The bigger the executional idea, the better Clouser liked it. If you could throw in a director such as Ridley Scott or a celebrity such as Stevie Wonder, all the better. But Chris never seemed one for the grit and grimble of day-to-day marketing, so it was a surprise indeed when he landed the big job at a company as challenging and complex as Bell Atlantic. He would need a crutch. And I was it.

As all this was going on, JWT began to experience life under Martin Sorrell. His person remained something of a mystery, but his intentions certainly did not. When he visited the San Francisco office for the first time, he never once mentioned the word "advertising." It seemed that he was only interested in looking at our books. I asked if he would like to meet the staff. He declined. I was prepared to show him our work. He demurred. We might just as well have been manufacturing corrugated cardboard. Or shopping baskets.

For more than a century, the symbols of the Thompson Company had been the owl and lantern – representing for generations of JWT clients and professionals the much-admired qualities of wisdom and enlightenment. But, when I attended one final U.S. manager's meeting before turning over the San Francisco reins to Steve, new president of JWT North America Ron Burns delivered a spirited sermon about increasing profits and presented each manager with a new symbol – the crystal statue of a shark. Martin Sorrell's hot breath was in the room.

Bringing me back to New York caused a brief "title" crisis. In companies the size of J. Walter Thompson, titles were often invented and proffered without regard to rhyme or reason. To those who valued face above common sense, what was on your business card was often as important as what was in your paycheck. It was all very silly. (At one board meeting, Joe O'Donnell and Chicago creative director Ralph Rydholm gave a hilarious presentation on the absurdity of Thompson's titles dressed as Emperor Napoleon and Lord Wellington.)

I had been a general manager out West, but I wasn't going to be a general manager here. And, in Jim Patterson, New York already had an executive creative director. Finally, in some smoke-filled room, it was decided Jim and I would be co-executive creative directors. This pleased neither of us, but since we were both equally peeved, it was adjudged to have been the wise decision.

I had to quickly assemble a team from Jim's spare parts to take on a tremendously complicated and very much in a hurry Bell Atlantic account. These people didn't know what to make of me, nor I them. Until I could sort out the various talents and egos, loyalties and commitment, it was a scorpion's mating dance. Creative Supervisor Frank Nicolo proved to be a savant -- diving into myriad details, sorting them into some semblance of order, and drawing a map for the rest of us.

Then there was the brilliant Linda Kaplan. Now among the most celebrated woman in advertising, then she was an eager-eyed wunderkind – always ready with a jingle and a smile and the owner of one of the brightest creative minds around. With a motley cast of supporting players, we were off to Washington to slay the beast.

And beast it was. Bell Atlantic was one company in name only. In reality, it was the foster parent of seven very parochial local telephone companies, each beholden as much to individual state authorities as they were to the corporation. The cultures of Bell of Pennsylvania, Chesapeake & Potomac Telephone, New Jersey Bell and the rest were rooted more in their differences than in what joined them in common. Each had their own Yellow Pages and business-to-business operations. Couple this with the explosion of new technologies (such as the controversial "Caller I.D"), corporate ventures into sidebar ventures such as aircraft leasing, and we had ourselves a communications gumbo.

Master politician Clouser had been hired to bring unity and

harmony to the internal marketing and advertising operation. In doing so, he manifested a curious management style. He really didn't have staff so much as he had followers. They didn't work for Chris; they attended to him. In the past and into the future, the same faces kept showing up in his entourage from Sprint to Bell Atlantic to Northwest to Burger King. Oh, there's Deanna again. And Charlie and Rick and Craig -- even Ed. Hail, hail, the gang's all here.

Working with this insular group, it was JWT's job to create advertising that would mollify individual state and local audiences, convinced that some evil force was trying to take away "my telephone company." This required a combination of finesse, guile and good old-fashioned arm-twisting.

With Linda and Frank handling the day-to-day operation, my fulltime job became Clouser. Off and on, and one way or the other, he would remain so for the rest of my days at Thompson.

35
Two Presidents and a Rascal

Clouser was easily bored. The steady stream of Bell Atlantic print ads and television commercials the group was turning out failed to keep him amused for very long. That we were successfully managing a very complex communications plan and deftly dealing with the capricious royalty of the various Bell Atlantic fiefdoms might have impressed most ad wonks. But Chris needed a new toy and went hearkening back to his Eagleton days.

"Let's do a 'get out the vote' commercial," he said to me early in October. Yes, 1990 was an election year, and, indeed, Bell Atlantic was the government's telephone company. But this seemed a bit off message and I told Chris so. Undeterred, he challenged me to "See what you can dream up. I've got lots of connections in the beltway." He wasn't through. "Oh, and I want to use that song *People Got to Be Free*...you know, the old Rascals' record."

It was like trying to construct a bird's nest out of shoelaces. But, as I was to learn, that's how Clouser adventures always began – with big ideas that didn't have shape and loose ends hanging out all over. He relied on me to make sense of it all and to tie everything together into neat little bundles of advertising.

So off I went, strategy be damned. Working with a droll art director from England named Roy Herbert, I began to form the basis of a commercial structure. The idea was to pick a single political contest of high interest somewhere in the Bell Atlantic area, and follow the candidates – Republican and Democrat – day after day, anywhere they took us – from fund raisers to stump speeches to whistle stops to kissing babies. We would show America at its "Grass Roots."

Backwards as this sounds, we hired a director before we had a storyboard or script. But history was on our side: Fred Levinson had shot Ronald Reagan's groundbreaking "Morning in America" film, so we knew he gave us every good chance of capturing the essence of the American political spirit. In scouring the electoral landscape for subject matter, we homed in on a particularly heated race in New Jersey between incumbent Democratic Senator Frank Lautenberg and his Republican challenger General Pete Dawkins (Army's famous Heisman Trophy winner for you college football fans). True to his beltway word, Clouser got us inside their campaigns and we spent the better part of two weeks shooting endless scenes of electioneering, conducted between countless dinners of rubber chicken and canned peas.

It was then that a few drinks between old friends changed everything. Clouser was carousing around D.C. with Jody Powell, President Jimmy Carter's onetime press secretary. Before the ice in their glasses had melted, they'd dealt Carter into our project. To balance things out, they secured the services of a Republican – former President Gerald Ford. Fred, Roy and I holed up in a roadside motel near Trenton to concoct a scenario for two Presidents. And a Rascal.

What you learn very quickly about Presidents – even ex ones – is that they don't come to you; you go to them. They don't abide by your schedule; you accommodate theirs. Now, all that is fine, unless you're footing the bill for a film crew of forty or fifty and are obliged to schlep them and their truckloads of equipment around three states for two weeks.

Our first stop was Miami, where Ford was scheduled to deliver a fundraising address in support of a local candidate. Our script called for him to appear at an outdoor rally and to say a few words. I wrote a simple line for him to memorize: "I'd like to thank the people of Bell Atlantic for helping get out the vote." My mistake.

The day of the filming (you can't say "shoot" when you're

around a President) dawned clear and cold. As we set up the lights and camera, we noticed that the Secret Service had positioned men with high-powered rifles on rooftops around the perimeter. When the President arrived, he was surrounded by a battalion of agents. Fred spent a few moments alone with him, describing the action, and going over the script.

When the camera began to roll, it was as if Chevy Chase had dropped by to do a sketch for *Saturday Night Live*.

"I'd like to help the people of..."

"Cut. One more time Mr. President."

"I'd like to Bell Atlantic the help..."

"Cut. Take your time Mr. President."

"I'd like to vote for the people..."

"Cut."

"Damn," the President said. There's just something awkward about the copy. Who wrote this?"

I walked up to the President, closely shadowed by a brace of Secret Service agents. After reading the line aloud to him a couple of times, I pep-talked him into believing he could get right it with one more try.

Actually, it took a few more tries, but the 38th President of the United States eventually spit out our words in some semblance of their original order.

Next stop was Plains, Georgia – home to Jimmy Carter and a helluva lot of peanuts. We were scheduled to "film" the President the next day in a nearby Americus grade school, Plains being too small to have schools of its own. It's also "dry" and Roy and I were in deep need of a beer after a dusty two-hour drive through farm country from the Columbus airport. To our great relief, there was one bar in Americus, tucked behind a sorry excuse of a motel, so hidden from sight that it took a couple of locals with a shotgun mounted in the rear window of their pick-up to lead us there.

We walked in to country music playing, a few couples line dancing and a long bar populated by weathered men with dirt under their fingernails. Whoever looked our way looked askance. We were obviously out of towners and the conversation quieted as we sat down. It took until the second beer, but the bartender eventually asked us what brought us to these parts.

"We're here to shoot, uh, film the President," I said. "Do you know him? How's he to work with?" Ears perked up.

"Sure," he said. "Everybody knows Jimmy. Jimmy's fine."

Roy and I had gone back to our beers and our own talking when I felt a tap on my shoulder.

"If y'all buy us drink, we'll tell you the truth about Jimmy." Three or four good ol' boys had gathered around.

"What'll you have?" I asked. This was an offer too good to refuse. For the price of a few bourbons, we'd get the straight scoop on Carter. It seems that everybody around Americus loved the President'a fun-loving brother and his Billy Beer, his homily-speaking mother Miss Lillian – even daughter Amy, who one Christmas famously asked Santa for a chain saw. But, Jimmy? Him they didn't like. And for the next couple of hours and a few more bourbons, we got an earful.

So it was with some trepidation that Roy and I showed up for the shoot the next morning. I filled Fred in on the previous night's conversation and we braced for the worst. Instead we met a man driving his own modest sedan, accompanied by one – just one – Secret Service agent. He was unfailingly polite, took direction willingly, charmed the children and was wrapped in two hours.

In this execution-driven film, the soundtrack would play a critical role and we still had Clouser's music to tend to. He'd expected us to just buy the rights to the original recording of *People Got to Be Free* and drop the needle. But, we explained to him, we needed to mix sound effects, on-camera dialogue and voiceover narration into the final track, and the only right course was to record from scratch.

As always, I called in Paul Hoffman, who flew from New York to Nashville to record Felix Cavaliere, one of the original Young Rascals. At their popular peak, there had been four Rascals. But, to the ear, there were only Felix and three guys named Joe. His was the distinctive voice and the only one America would recognize. (That was fortunate, because the other three Rascals hadn't spoken to Felix in years.)

Backing Felix with Nashville session players, we produced a track that sounded more like the record than the record, yet had all the necessities of timing and flexibility we needed for the commercial.

As for the narration, a gravely voice added just the right grace note. Because the script was written in lofty tones, it demanded more nuance than can be expected from a standard voiceover announcer. So, once again, we took Clouser to school and sold him on the wisdom of paying a premium for the whiskey tenor of Jason Robards.

"Grass Roots" turned out to be a triumph by most measures. It was praised by the press and won its share of awards. But, like most triumphs, it came with a price. We had created a monster in Chris Clouser and deserve blame for that. Now that he'd tasted the thrill of working with one of his boyhood music heroes, Felix Cavaliere, and could call the famous Jason Robards by his first name, Chris fell for show business real bad. What little regard he'd had for strategy before, now disappeared completely. All he wanted from here on were ever bigger and splashier entertainments.

In the coming months, that would take us to a galaxy far, far away.

36
The Million-Dollar Check

Actually, Clouser was only half mad. His penchant for entertainment and glamour gave us the opportunity to produce a body of work that clearly stood out from the dreary sameness of 1990s telephone advertising. After the success of the vote spot, Jason Robards became the distinctive voice of all Bell Atlantic commercials, and we wrote to his cadence. We designed a series of :60 films starring the likes of Roberta Flack and Helen Hayes, which celebrated the lives of native sons and daughters "in the Bell Atlantic Neighborhood," giving each of the component companies their moment to shine. Linda did a series of spots with Alex Haley, still riding on the crest of the popularity of *Roots*. Following up one of his crazier ideas, Clouser and I sat down for an exploratory meeting with Henry Kissinger.

It wasn't long before we dipped our toes into sponsored programming. In the fall of 1990 Bell Atlantic presented "To Be Free: The National Literacy Honors," hosted by President and Mrs. George H.W. Bush. The Bushes were nice enough to loan us the White House for the black-tie evening and to make a grand entrance down red-carpeted stairs as the Marine Corps band played *Hail to the Chief.*

This only whetted Clouser's appetite. In his *Hallmark Hall of Fame* days, he had become enamored of high quality, advertiser-driven, branded television specials. Now he wanted to create such a property for Bell Atlantic. "Think me up a 'Hall of Fame,'" he said, and handed me an open wallet and a clean canvas.

I bought a ticket to Hollywood. Figuring there must be a fertile crop of ideas germinating around the film and broadcast communities, I headed for L.A. and my old colleague Farlan Myers. Farlan had once been head of JWT's Hollywood office and had a Rolodex to choke a William Morris agent. He didn't disappoint. For the next week, we heard pitches from studios and networks for specials, dramas and events, oh my. But, in the end, everything sounded a bit been-there-seen-that. There was nothing to make the blood rush for a high-tech, forward-looking communications company.

The kernal of an idea originally grew from an article I'd stuffed in a briefcase full of airplane reading. Even then, the national conversation was all about the approaching millennium and whether the clocks would stop running and life as we know it would cease to exist. The fact is, the more one read, the more it was evident that, while no one knew exactly what the future looked like, everyone sure as hell wanted to know. Struck by that notion somewhere over Kansas, I pulled out my trusty Olivetti (no laptops, yet) and began to tap out a treatment.

"What if," it began, "we were to produce a 10-part series of annual programs -- beginning in 1991 and extending up to the year 2000 -- examining every aspect of 21st century life – from drugs to war; from technology to disease; from over-population to religion?" And so, the idea of *Bell Atlantic's Millennium* was born. Of course, thinking it up was one thing, pulling it off was quite another. It was time, as Joe O'Donnell would say, to "throw long." Who had the vision for such a project? And, who had the box office appeal to attract a major network?

I called Farlan. "Do you have George Lucas and Steven Spielberg in your Rolodex?"

"It won't do you any good," he said. "They get a hundred offers a day." Then he spent a few teachable moments giving me an earful about not wasting his or their time on a half-baked long shot and blah, blah, blah. Then, as always, he said: "Send me your treatment and I'll see what I can do."

What he did was call Sid Ganis, Lucas's longtime executive producer. Though not overly encouraging, Ganis said he'd get the treatment into George's hands.

"Bill." It was my secretary, Deb Groth. "Would you have time to take a call from a Mr. Lucas?"

Indeed, it was the mega director of *Star Wars*. He wanted to know if I could come out and meet with him at the Skywalker

Ranch. Skywalker is a nice little spread of almost 5,000 acres, tucked into the Nicasio area of Marin County California. A sprawling scenic and architectural wonder, it serves as a campus for filmmakers, complete with multiple motion picture editing and screening rooms and a state-of-the-art scoring studio. The Victorian-inspired Main House is Lucas' residence and meeting area. Just off the foyer, a research library of stunning proportions sits in natural light beneath a 40-foot stained glass dome. If you have $100 million laying around, you can have a Skywlker Ranch, too.

Lucas walked into the meeting room as I was admiring the actual robotic hand of C3P0, R2D2's sidekick in *Star Wars*. (In Lucas' myth-filled world, it's disarming to learn that R2D2 got his name from the canister of movie dailies in which he makes his first appearance: Reel 2, Day 2.) Lucas was wearing his usual flannel shirt and blue jeans. I felt overdressed.

It was a remarkable conversation and very one sided. In retrospect, it shouldn't have been surprising that Lucas was thinking along the same futuristic lines we were and, in fact, had assigned Ranch researchers to study a number of the very subjects we had suggested in the treatment. If we went forward, he proposed that he both direct and produce the first program and then act as executive producer for the other nine. We agreed to hold a potluck meeting in two weeks time. He would bring an outline of the first program, I would bring Clouser, and Clouser would bring his checkbook.

"Millennium I" got off to a promising start. On the appointed meeting day, our small traveling party was given the full

Skywalker Ranch treatment. After Lucas made his outline presentation, we had lunch in the Solarium, prepared by Lucas' personal chef. At day's end, Clouser left duly charmed and lighter by $1,000,000. With this seed money, Lucas hired a full time line producer and opened a production office. We were in business.

What happened next certainly begged an explanation, though none was ever given. Four months into production, Clouser called. "It's off," he said. "Tell George I'm sorry and he can keep the money, but it's off." No matter how I tried, I couldn't budge him into elaboration or reconsideration.

This was not a message for the phone. So I flew to San Francisco and drove the 60 miles to Skywalker to meet with Lucas personally. Though he was clearly disappointed, he handed me a $1,000,000 check on my way out the door. "Tell Chris that if I can have the idea, we're even." In the way these things go, my idea had been sold twice in four months for $1,000,000 each time -- and not one dollar ever found its way into J. Walter Thompson's pocket.

We now had a habit on our hands. Just a few weeks earlier, Clouser had pulled the plug on a project with Sir Ridley Scott. The famed director of such blockbusters as "Blade Runner," "The Alienist" and "Gladiator," Ridley had agreed to shoot a series of commercials for Bell Atlantic based on a Roy Herbert concept called "Computer Heads." But, first, he wanted to sit down with the client and agency to discuss his vision. A meeting was scheduled for a Saturday morning in Los Angeles in Ridley's suite at The Four Seasons Hotel. Even though he'd flown all night from London, he was bright, friendly and ready to dive into the concepts. Clouser was late, and Ridley couldn't help but begin an animated discussion.

The phone rang. It was for me. "I'm not coming," Clouser said. "Apologize, but tell Ridley we're going to have to cancel the shoot."

To his credit, Scott didn't throw us out of his room – as any normal diva would have. But, in the Hollywood community, where one's word and follow-through are currency, the color of our money and the value of our promises took another Clouser hit.

It's as true in an advertising agency creative department as it is on a football team: if you have two starting quarterbacks, you have none. And during the year it became evident that Jim Patterson and I were one quarterback too many – especially when Patterson insisted on calling all the plays. (Including one in which he phoned to ask if I would handle a ticklish personnel situation with a young art director – who also happened to be his live-in girl friend. It was the raise-giving season and she wasn't getting one. Jim wanted me to break the news. I didn't dignify the request with a response.)

Much to our mutual relief, the Company intervened. After years of gnashing their collective teeth over the long-festering Agnew situation out West, they "suddenly" decided to act. They first made sure Clouser was comfortable in the creative leadership of Linda Kaplan on Bell Atlantic, then threw me an extravagant goodbye party, slapped me on the back and handed me a one-way ticket to L.A.

37
A Fool's Errand

I was dispatched to Los Angeles under false pretenses, as-suming the Trojan Horse position of Head of the West. With the tacit understanding that I would leave him alone, Steve Darland in San Francisco agreed to report to me on paper, and it was under-stood that Jim Agnew and I would share the manager's chair in Los Angeles. The obvious but unspoken reason behind this epic ruse was to get rid of Agnew, whose style and manner stuck in the craw of just about every Thompson executive east of Lake Tahoe. I would spend a few months getting to know the L.A. clients and sizing up the staff. Then, at a moment of New York's choosing, Jim would be invited to take his career elsewhere.

You could make the case that we should have left L.A. alone. Jim's compensation arrangements with key clients were a bit dicey and the office was a little over extended in real estate, but as a manager for that market, Agnew was straight out of central casting. He played a fine game of Beverly Hills tennis and knew the maitre'd at Spago. He had a talented beach boy of a creative director in Denny Kuhr, with whom he had successfully teamed at McCann-Erickson in a previous life. Agnew may have made man-agement queasy and his office may not have operated like other

Thompson offices, but in it's own quirky way, L.A. worked okay.
It. had long been an anomaly in the JWT universe. For
decades, it stood in the shadow of the Hollywood office, which
produced some of the most famous radio programs in broadcast
history. The Hollywood office gave America Bing Crosby, Bob
Hope and Ozzie & Harriet. For its part, the Los Angeles office
gave America Bob Haldeman, Ron Ziegler and Dwight Chapin --
who famously moved on to the White House, Watergate and jail.
(Evidently, Haldeman had used his Thompson years as on-the-job
training for politics. Long after he had vacated the premises, the
JWT conference room was robbed of all its audio-visual equipment. In making repairs, workman discovered an elaborate eaves-
dropping system that connected directly through to what had once
been Haldeman's office.)

I hadn't even received my building pass and parking card
when bad news landed on my desk with an ominous thud. We had
just been fired by 20th Century Fox, which erased a $29 million
chunk of billing from the books. Ignoring the advice of those closest to the account, Agnew took too firm a stand during contract ne-
gotiations and had his head handed to him. That left the office
with only two major pieces of business – Bally's Health & Tennis
and Vons Supermarkets – and a bunch of other ones that just kind
of straggled along.

My presence didn't escape notice and *AdWeek* was quick to
the news. "Los Angeles…is in for a change," Kathy Brown wrote.
"The L.A. office had been headed by executive vp/general manager Jim Agnew, labeled the 'quintessential account man' and executive vp/cd Denny Kuhr, the easy-going creative. (Both are

expected to stay on, though Agnew has been trailed by departure rumors.)

"Lane, tagged by one associate as the 'antithesis of Agnew' ... is not afraid to ruffle feathers to pound an idea into a client's head." The prose was a bit purple, but Kathy had it right. I'd been brought in once again to shake things up.

Mexicana Airlines was on its way out the door as I arrived. During my first few days, I attended a so called "save the business" presentation. There I came face to face with as curious a set of characters as a writer of fiction could conjure. The loudest voice in the room was Jim O'Donnell, who ran the Houston half of Mexicana's marketing team. O'Donnell was to airlines as Big Ed Carter was to telephone. An itinerant V.P. of marketing, he'd stay just long enough at any one place to challenge the status quo, devise great plans and rise like Icarus too close to the sun.

His counterpart on the other side of the border was Pepe Kuri, Latin right down to his loins, who was clearly not pleased with how the meeting was going. Denny was presenting brand work and the client was preaching retail. Agnew was defending Denny and they were all but ignoring him.

I took a chance and butted in. "What if...?" I said and "How about?" They leaned forward, amused that anyone from our side of the table would listen to their point of view. I apologized for being new and asked them for two weeks to put together a presentation to address their concerns. Pepe Kuri reached into his pocket and drew out a lucky gold piece. It was his bet that I would fail. I took the bet.

We proceeded to do some rousing good work in the coming

months and to manage a few dicey personnel issues. It was clear from the first meeting that the current L.A. account team needed a talent infusion, so we served up a bright young lady named Janine Perkel from our internal staff to handle the business day to day. O'Donnell countered with a handpicked outsider he knew from Continental Airlines named Mindy Balgrosky. Remembering the lesson learned from my San Francisco experience, when I'd failed to hire the friend of client Jim Gordon and thereby put the Chevron account in play, I bent to O'Donnell's wishes. As Mindy – who was to become a great friend -- tells the story, my exact quote was "Just hire the bitch."

A letter from Client O'Donnell to Burt Manning pretty much summed up our contribution:

"Since you're the usual recipient of bad news, I thought it fair that you be the first to hear the good news for a change…I know of nothing that more severely tests an agency's infrastructure than a flat-out retail crisis like this one, and you have every right to be proud of your people. Overall, I have not seen any team per- form more professionally, effectively and cheerfully while moving immense amounts of the product without doing anything to harm the product's image."

Nestled in a shoebox somewhere in my attic, Pepi Kuri's gold coin shines as evidence of our success.

Denny Kuhr had single-handedly made Vons a showcase account. He created a series of folksy television commercials fea- turing president Bill Davila. They not only made Vons #1 in a very competitive category, but also made Davila famous enough to run for mayor.

By far the dominant account was Bally's Health & Tennis, which contributed fully half of the agency's revenue. Tremendously work intensive, it operated on the same basic principle as had Sprint: try to get enough eager new customers to walk in the front door every day to cover for the loss of disgruntled ones who were walking out the back. Again, Denny Kuhr was a star, creating funny, compelling commercials featuring the likes of Cher and Raquel Welch.

But Bally's was also a mare's nest. Although its billings were $80 million in measured media, Agnew had accepted contract terms that returned only $4 million to the agency. Beyond that, Jim agreed to allow Bally's to pay 60-90 days late, in effect letting them float along for months at a time on Thompson money.

Which brings us to the day-to-day client, Arthur Quinby. Quinby had been imported from JWT Chicago to run the Bally's business and grew to despise Agnew over time. Health & Tennis president Don Wyldman (whose name had a sort of Dickensian truth to it) thought so much of Arthur that he brought him over to the client side. Quinby took special delight in torturing Agnew, especially after Jim fired a talented account person, who just happened to be Mrs. Quinby. To review the bidding: bad compensation agreement, dangerous financial exposure, and a client with a motive for revenge.

If it hadn't been for Pat Rogge, the whole thing might have fallen apart. Rogge is the dictionary definition of the client service man. He will climb ev'ry mountain, ford ev'ry stream and follow ev'ry rainbow in the performance of his duties. Knowing that Wyldman was a health and fitness fanatic, Rogge, a two-pack-a-

212

day man, gave up smoking. He began to run 2-3 miles a day and looked as fit as, well, a Pat Rogge could look. He wasn't afraid to be tough when he needed to be -- but smart, fair and ever-loyal Rogge doggedly won the client's affection and trust.

Things were going according to plan. During my first months in L.A., I'd spent a considerable bit of time with Quinby. (As it turns out, as young men, we had attended one of the Thompson training seminars together at Troutbeck in Duchess County, New York, and had struck up a collegial friendship.) For all intents and purposes, I'd assumed day-to-day responsibility for Del Taco and Mexicana. The client at McDonnell Douglas, Jim Barker, was a college classmate of mine. Ron Burns, head of JWT/USA had made a couple of forays to L.A. for private dinners with Quinby and Bill Davila. It was time to pull the trigger.

Denny Kuhr and Pat Rogge were critical to the agency's success going forward and I took them aside separately. Explaining what was about to happen, I threw the blame entirely on New York. "Deal's done," I said. "Nothing you or I can do about it." Assuring them that the two of them had the full endorsement of Company management, I stressed how important they were to the future of the L.A. office and asked for their support. It was given, if grudgingly, and we arranged an off-site meeting to orchestrate the change.

Burns would fly to L.A. on D-Day minus one. After hours, he would meet with Agnew and give him the news. The next morning, every employee would find a memo on his or her desk announcing that I would succeed Jim. Burns and I would already be in a hired car, moving from client to client to deliver the news personally. Denny would remain behind to deal with any internal unrest. Poor Denny. Thank goodness he had a refrigerator in his office stocked with Budweisers.

It was not a day I would choose to repeat. While Arthur Quinby was pleased at the news, Bill Davila was less so. He liked Jim and didn't like change – few clients do when it involves their agency. His manner was frosty, but he calmed some when assured that Denny would continue as his creative director and we would keep his account team in place. Del Taco and McDonnell Douglas seemed impressed that JWT management had flown all the way out from New York to talk to them face to face. Mexicana had forgotten Agnew existed.

That afternoon, I called an all-staff meeting to explain the change and to answer questions. It was not a happy group. That evening, when I went down to fetch my car from the employee parking lot, I discovered a large, deep scratch across the driver's side door which extended a good way along the rear quarter panel, evidently made with an angry key. It was no accident.

38
All about the Benjamins

As we had shown we could do in San Francisco, we set about trying to make a true J. Walter Thompson office out of Los Angeles. We might have succeeded, too, had Martin Sorrell been able to control his lust for corporate takeovers. With Pat Rogge as deputy general manager in charge of internal operations, we established a program of regular strategic review boards and instituted standard practices in an attempt to turn what had been a rather seat-of-the-pants operation into a more disciplined unit. A new management committee was formed, with members held strictly accountable for the performance of their businesses.

Finances were a mess across the board. Of immediate concern was Mexicana Airlines and its saddleback management. The Houston marketing operation, headed by O'Donnell, was in charge of ordering up advertising. The Mexico City office and Pepe Kuri were in charge of paying for it. While Houston did a mighty good job with the ordering part, Mexico City had an annoying habit of stuffing our invoices in a drawer.

After weeks of being told "the check is in the mail," I told them not to send it. I would come to Mexico City and pick it up in person. "That won't be necessary," they said.

"No problema," I said and hopped a jet. Arriving in the reception area on their executive floor at 10:00 one morning (as I had been invited to do), I asked for a Mr. Saenz, whom I had been informed would have our check.

"Senor Saenz is in a meeting," I was told.

"That's fine. I'll wait."

At about noon, I tiptoed up to the receptionist and asked when Senor Saenz would be out of his meeting.

"I'm sorry. But Senor Saenz has left for lunch." Backdoor Saenz had given me the slip.

At about 2:00, I asked if Senor Sanchez had returned.

"Yes," the receptionist said. "But he's meeting with the president."

"Does he know I'm here?"

"Oh, yes. He say's he's sorry, but if you wish to come back tomorrow, he'll understand."

"Please tell Senor Saenz that if the check isn't in my hands by 4:00 today, I'm walking through his door and I don't care who he's with."

At about 3:55, an aide to Saenz handed me a check for several hundred thousand dollars of Mexicana's money. By the time I landed in Los Angeles, they had stopped payment.

Meanwhile, across the pond, Martin Sorrell had again strapped on his acquisition boots, this time setting his sights on Ogilvy & Mather. That didn't please the iconic David Ogilvy, who publicly referred to Sorrell as "that odious little shit." As Martin was running around to lenders in search of hostile takeover cash, the moneymen demanded to see JWT's books. It was then that the ticking time bomb that was Bally's Health & Tennis was exposed.

That odious little shit hit the fan.

Bally's owed J. Walter Thompson $12 million, an amount that grew with each media-buying day. It didn't help matters that rumors of their possible bankruptcy were floating around the financial press. Somehow, Pat got Wyldman and Arthur to agree to cut JWT a check for $4 million and New York backed off a little -- but only a little -- and only until the check bounced. Pat got that news on a car phone as he was driving his BMW along Wilshire Boulevard. He ran into the car in front of him.

Unbeknownst to Pat or me, Martin flew from London to Bally's headquarters in Chicago and, with along with Manning, confronted their management. He demanded that they come current. When Bally's refused, reminding Martin that Agnew had agreed to 90-day terms, Sorrell ordered us to immediately cease buying airtime and to lock up the creative. The only way Bally's could get back on the air -- to feed the belly of their beast -- was to agree to a strict pay down schedule. They had no choice. In their business, going dark for any extended period was suicide.

It was a precarious time. Even though the current onerous payment arrangement had been dictated from upstairs and afar, our dealings with the local Health & Tennis clients couldn't help but show the strain. Denny continued to edit new versions of the popular and effective Raquel Welch commercials, one or two at a time as money was repaid. Pat continued to hold Quinby's hand. (I believe it might have been about now that Rogge took up smoking again.) We'd managed to keep a press lid on the delicate nature of the Bally's relationship.

But the lie could't last. Yes, Bally's paid down the debt. Yes, we locked up the creative and only released it a little at a time as the money came in. Yes, we eventually recovered every dollar. And, yes, at the end of it all, they fired us.

We were in real trouble. An immediate, across-the-board layoff was staring us in the face. The local advertising press was proclaiming our demise. Remaining clients demanded evidence that we would still be able to adequately service their accounts. I assigned Pat the unenviable task of seeing what it would take to get out of our real estate lease.

If anything, we over served Vons. We shifted a number of our brightest people, now freed up from other responsibilities, to their account. While continuing do winning creative, we made several presentations of brand-building ideas, hoping somehow to boost billings.

Alas, it was all to no avail. One Monday morning, I received a call from Bill Davila asking if I would join him at Vons' Glendale headquarters at noon on that Wednesday – alone. It took me about an hour to get there (it takes an hour to get anywhere in L.A.) but I arrived on time and was ushered into Davila's office.

"We're sorry to hear of the trouble you're having with your other accounts," he began. But the J. Walter Thompson we see now just isn't the same J. Walter Thompson we hired. I'm afraid we have no choice but to move the business." He handed me a formal letter of termination.

I guess it took me the usual hour to get back to the office, but it seemed a whole lot longer. My knuckles were white. I really didn't see how we could go on. Our two major sources of revenue were gone, and the remaining accounts certainly couldn't sustain an office of our size.

And then I got one of those out-of-the-blue calls that can save a day. It was Chris Clouser and he was in town and wanted to talk to me about his Big New Job. He picked me up at the JWT offices on Wilshire and we drove to The Grill in Beverly Hills, parking Chris's car in a public garage just down the block.

Over many drinks and one sundown, Clouser announced that he was to be the new V.P of marketing for Northwest Airlines and, just as with Bell Atlantic, wanted me to handle the account. Did I want to be on the phone with him when he told Manning? Would I move to New York?

I had other ideas. Since Northwest headquarters were in Minneapolis, and Minneapolis isn't that much farther from Los

Angeles as a DC-9 flies than it is from New York, why couldn't we handle the account out of L.A.? Without telling him so, it was just about the only way we could save the office.

As we plotted, the time for his redeye flight grew near. We settled the check and went to fetch his car – only to find that the garage was closed for the night. Clouser's car was locked inside the garage and his briefcase and wallet were locked inside the car. What's an agency guy to do? I borrowed a hundred from the bartender at the Grill, called a car service and got Chris to the airport. His smile and a lie or two got him on a plane to Minneapolis without I.D. In those days, security at LAX had never heard of Al Qaeda.

About a week later, Clouser sat down with Denny, Rogge and me in Los Angeles. He asked us to help him do some thinking on a confidential Northwest project – a proposed merger with British Airways. With each meeting, the reality of this being our account seemed more promising. I had gone so far as to approach a recently deposed Jim O'Donnell (the Icarus factor) to join us as account director.

Who knows who pulled the plug? Manning? Martin? Clouser himself? All I can be sure of is that I was summoned to New York and told that, yes, J. Walter Thompson would be announced as the agency of record for Northwest, and, yes I would run it, but that the account would be handled out of the New York office. I would move immediately east and the remaining L.A. accounts and staff would be folded under San Francisco management.

As I said, you could make the case that we should have left L.A. alone.

39
Deja Vu

Once again, New York. Once again, Clouser. But, instead of traveling every week to cosmopolitan Washington, D.C., where Bell Atlantic had been headquartered, I now found myself on a weekly yo-yo to Minneapolis, home to Northwest Airlines and Spam. While Minneapolis is a lot of nice things, cosmopolitan isn't one of them. They fancy ice fishing there, and the opening of walleye season is cause for civic celebration. (Minnesota is first among the United States in the number of fishing licenses issued annually.)

Northwest had been around since the 1920s. In his barn-storming days, Charles Lindbergh had flown the Northwest mail route to and from Chicago. Somewhere in the 30s, they figured out how to fly to Asia via the Arctic Circle without falling out of the sky and gained some notoriety for that. However, that didn't exactly make them preferred. They were known far and wide as "Northworst Airlines" and strived mightily to live down to that reputation every day. (On one of my first early-morning trips to Minneapolis, breakfast was what is fondly referred to in the Army as "shit on a shingle.") It didn't help matters that three Northwest Airlines pilots had recently been convicted of collectively downing at least 15 rum and cokes and 6 pitchers of beer just before getting behind the controls of a 727 with 91 passengers on board for a flight between Minneapolis and Fargo.

But change was afoot. A couple of hotshot executives from Marriott and Disney named Gary Wilson and Al Checchi took their combined corporate gelt and led a leveraged buyout of the airline. They landed in Minneapolis hell bent on turning around its reputation. Clouser was brought in to lead the marketing charge and, on behalf of J. Walter Thompson, I was to be his sharp sword.

Effecting organizational change is always a challenge, but Northwest provided a daunting test. Its employees were nice people, ya betcha, but their culture was decidedly civil service. It's as if they'd been issued a little rule book to be followed to the letter; from precisely 9:00 in the morning until exactly 5:00 at night; from the first day they were hired until the day they began collecting their pensions. They would gather at midday in the company cafeteria, many of the women knitting scarves and sweaters. Looking out a conference room window in the late afternoons, one could see cafeteria employees hauling great troughs of leftover food out into the wide-open fields behind headquarters to feed the local fauna. This might be the only wildlife population on earth to dine regularly on macaroni and cheese.

Early on, I was made part of a committee, chaired by Northwest's president John Dasburg, charged with drawing up a corporate mission statement. We toiled for what seemed like weeks. Everyone's opinion, including that of the night watchman, found its way into the final draft. The result was an olio of blather. (On the day we finished, I was riding in the elevator of a nondescript airport hotel when I noticed their management had proudly posted a mission statement on the back wall. If I'd simply swapped that one for Northwest's, I'll bet big money that no one at headquarters – let alone a consumer – would have noticed the difference.)

There have been times when I've said to a client "advertising is the last thing you should do." I'll recommend that, if their product and service offering comes up short as compared to competition, they get things right in-house before going public. According to the old adage, nothing kills a bad product quicker than great advertising.

Certainly, this advice could have applied to Northwest. But I sensed that this confluence of history and circumstances required a different approach; that this was the time for Northwest to put a stake in the ground, to make a big promise, then invite its people to go out and make it true.

So, I asked for and received separate audiences with Checchi, Wilson and Dasburg. I told them to close their eyes to Northwest's shortcomings and to dream a big dream. "What do you hope to be?" I asked each of them. "At day's end, what do you want people to believe about you?

From out of their wishes, a campaign came. At bottom, they wanted Northwest to be a "smart" airline -- not a flashy one or a warm fuzzy one – but an airline intelligent people choose. People who "get it." People who "know how." People who know how to fly.

This would not be an easy trick to pull off. In order to fly anywhere on Northwest, one usually had to start from or pass through its hubs in Detroit and Minneapolis -- in general, not an attractive prospect. (Dasburg tried to make lemonade out of these geographic lemons by proclaiming territorial pride: "They're cold. They're dark. And they're ours.")

The Northwest advertising group had never seen executions as ambitious as those we brought them. The launch spot was big budget and star driven, featuring celebrities famous for knowing

222

how to "fly." Olympic ice skater Nancy Kerrigan could do a triple jump, hanging in the air for seconds at a time. Art Monk, a hall of fame receiver for the Washington Redskins, was known for his gravity-defying catches. The diminutive NBA star Spud Webb could rise in the air and dunk over humans twice his size. The surprise ending had Superman Christopher Reeve eschewing his tights and cape to ride on Northwest Airlines. He was to put on his Clark Kent glasses and deliver the theme line. As he was about to shoot his scene, we received word from Reeve's dressing room that he refused to wear the glasses for the scene. I was sent by Clouser to reason with him. "Without the glasses, the bit doesn't work," I said, stepping all over the obvious. "I'm a serious actor," he said, taking himself far too seriously.

"This is Superman, for chrissakes," I said, "not Hamlet." "I won't do the glasses," he said finally. And he didn't.

Linda Kaplan and Fred Thaler composed rousing theme music. Our announcer was voice of God, James Earl Jones. (During a long recording session, I once asked James if he considered his to be the voice of God. No, no," he said from WAY DOWN THERE. "That's Walter Cronkite.") To direct, we selected the young maker of future blockbusters such as "Armageddon" and "Pearl Harbor," Michael Bay. With wires and rigs and the odd stunt double, the set was designed to make people fly.

The commercial, as well as Northwest's bold new attitude created some noise, though we took a few shots. "Hear that new Northwest Airlines slogan 'Some People Just Know How to Fly?'" Jay Leno said one night on *The Tonight Show*. "Well...(pause for affect)...I *certainly* hope so."

As for Clouser, the danger signs of a man striding toward

megalomania began to appear more frequently. Before every commercial shoot, he took to insisting that we arrange a dinner to include just him and the director -- no producer, no account person, no me. That led to him dictating his own directorial choices, thereby crossing the line between a client's privilege and an agency's responsibility. He would call JWT's Farlan Myers directly, ask him for the names of certain talent agents, then negotiate deals with celebrities all by himself. Advertising became his own private playground and, every so often, he would invite us to come over and share his toys.

As a result, we ended up with an odd assortment of commercials based on one man's proclivities, without regard to strategy or any defined, consistent message. How else do you explain a year's collection of spots that included a paraplegic wheelchair racer named Deanna Sodoma, wounded ice skater Nancy Kerrigan (on behalf of "Toys for Tots"), and a cross-country tour with the Neville Brothers?

Since the Felix Cavaliere days at Bell Atlantic, Clouser had used his advertising perch as a personal jukebox. At his direction, we created an on-going radio music campaign featuring his favorite artists from the 60s and 70s. Over the course of several years, we recorded tracks with B.B. King, Isaac Hayes, The Neville Brothers, Dr. John, The Four Tops, Tony Bennett, Phoebe Snow, Delbert McClinton and Mavis Staples, among others. But not for Northwest commercials, modern America wouldn't have heard Foreigner's aging lead singer Lou Gramm or Mark Farner of Grand Funk Railroad, nor realized they were still alive.

Things were about to become even more complicated. Clouser decided that "Some People Just Know How to Fly" would

224

make a fine worldwide campaign. Until this time, the many ports of call where Northwest did business had created country-specific advertising, taking into account the market-to-market vagaries of language and culture. It would be a mistake, Clouser was told by his country managers, to try and homogenize the advertising – especially among the ethnically diverse nations of Asia.

Of course, Clouser ignored their advice.

"Make it happen," he told me.

40
Sushi Diplomacy

I flew to Tokyo, where all hell broke loose. I'd asked the creative directors of the JWT Asia offices to meet me there to discuss how to make "Some People" work in their areas, only to discover that no two of them could agree on lunch, let alone on an advertising approach. While Thompson overseas general managers and multi-national account directors had long been internationalist in their thinking and cross-cultural in their outlook, creative directors tended to be local and to carry with them their own jingoistic chauvinism. The Japanese didn't trust the Thais; the Filipinos didn't have much use for the Hong Kong Chinese; and nobody liked the Koreans.

The one opinion they held in common was that I was the

enemy. I'd been sent by the Great White Father Clouser to colonize them. What in the hell does someone from New York know about a consumer in Seoul, anyway? Koeke-san from Tokyo was the most vocal.

"Your line does not translate," she said, to a chorus of bobbleheads. I was to learn that the Asians would always hide behind language when trying to get their way.

"Let's not be literal, here," I began. "Forget the words. Translate the spirit. Certainly the notions of being smart and an insider are qualities understood and admired universally. Besides, a customer on Northwest airlines is not a local but an international traveler. Let's not focus on everybody's cultural differences. Let's figure out what traits they share." A nice speech delivered to blank stares.

That night, Koeke took us all to her neighborhood sushi bar, casual and authentic, not a tourist place at all. A lot of sake and a few lusty rounds of karaoke got the conversation going in a way that the long day's meeting had not. The evening ended with me asking for their best thinking. If, after sincere effort, they all concluded that one world campaign would not work, I would carry their alternate solutions forward to Clouser and attempt to win him over to their point of view.

We tugged back and forth across the Pacific for two weeks. As I expected, the creative directors ultimately concluded that "Some People" would not work in their countries. I picked up the phone and called Koeke.

"Koeke-san," I said. "Before you tell me 'no,' go back and give me your best shot."

226

The next day, a fax from Koeke landed on my desk. There was only one sentence on the page -- a translation: "Some People Have Wings in their Hearts." It was brilliant, of course, and provided a creative path for the others to follow. Having slight variations from country to country to allow for cultural idiosyncrasy (and pride of authorship) proved an easy sell to Clouser and gave him great confidence that J. Walter Thompson could indeed orchestrate a coordinated effort around the world.

Thus began a series of international adventures, mostly having to do with the merger and coalition fever then infecting the aviation industry. Foreign carriers wanted greater entré into the United States. Northwest offered them that. Though strong to Asia, Northwest itched to expand into Europe, and looked to the continent to find a partner. Secret courtships were ardently pursued, almost always falling apart long before the altar, tail fin ego tending to get in the way. In these discussions, neither carrier was wont to give up its name. The only solutions palatable to both sides usually involved coming up with some sort of hybrid name or an entirely new one altogether.

It was on just such a mission that Clouser and I found ourselves in London. We were scheduled to brainstorm in total secrecy with representatives of British Airways on what a combined British and Northwest airlines might look and sound like. Meeting at JWT's 40 Berkeley Square offices, we spent two days coming up with a mind-numbing set of possibilities. At the beginning of the third day, I was scheduled to catch a plane back to New York for a client dinner that night. But enough progress had been made for them to ask me to stay – with the enticing promise that British would book me on the Concorde later in the afternoon. Indeed they did and I enjoyed the remarkable experience of taking off from London and arriving in New York at exactly the same hour.

A few months later, in Amsterdam, we barked up a more promising tree. Northwest had been approached by KLM to see if a fit could be had. This time, I took along Rory Phoenix, an art director from my San Francisco days, whom I had recently hired in New York. Again we holed up in secret, conjuring on names and livery. During coming months, the KLM romance would persist, eventually resulting, if not in an out-and-out merger, in joint marketing and advertising programs.

All this merger stuff was compromised by Northwest's precarious financial circumstance, word of which was leaking out all over. Because of their route structure, a severe recession in Asia had compromised their revenues to a degree not felt by competitors. A sudden and dramatic increase in fuel prices hit them squarely in their long-haul wallets. Their only course of survival was to approach their employees for wage and benefit concessions and their suppliers for any sort of price relief they could negotiate.

At that time, Northwest was the most unionized airline in a heavily unionized industry. It complicated matters that each of their major employee groups belonged to a different one. The 9,000 flight attendants were teamsters, a particularly militant group. The 27,000 baggage handlers, ground personnel and mechanics were machinists. The cockpit crews, as members of the Airline Pilots Association, had a very vocal and aggressive group all their own. The warring parties faced off – waiting, waiting, waiting for the others to blink. No one wanted to give in first.

Frankly, in their shortsighted way, no one wanted to give in at all.

At first, Clouser thought that the best way to deal with the intransigent unions was to sweet talk them with advertising. So, we found ourselves doing a series of commercials that made Northwest employees appear as so many Father Flannigan's and Mother Theresas. A flight attendant who knew how to sign made a deaf passenger feel comfortable and welcome. Through our lens, Northwest mechanics delivered more Toys for Tots than Santa himself.

The unions weren't buying this tack one bit. They responded by taking out a series of newspaper ads with scathing denunciations of Northwest management. In a move that wasn't in the best interest of anybody, Clouser decided to fight back. I became part of a group that spent long nights designing "reverse attack" ads. It was a pissing contest neither side could win.

Events eventually proceeded to High Noon. Northwest announced that, if it did not receive almost $900 million in concessions from the unions, it would be forced to declare bankruptcy. In a counter move, the unions demanded stock ownership and several seats on the Northwest board. In addition, they demanded that Northwest owners, lenders and suppliers kick in more than $300 million as a sign of good faith.

One of those suppliers was J. Walter Thompson. In the spirit of helping a troubled client in a moment of need, JWT was asked to reduce their commission rate to 10% for the foreseeable future. Burt Manning swallowed hard. Martin Sorrell dug in. But they couldn't stop the downward tumble of events.

41
The Camel's Nose

The moment the advertising industry began to surrender control over its own destiny can be traced to 1962 when Fred Papert and his cohorts at Papert Koenig and Lois sold their souls to a stock exchange. Little PKL was soon followed into public ownership by the big boys at Doyle Dane, Grey, J. Walter Thompson, McCann Erickson and, eventually, Young & Rubicam. Going public made the executive elite at these agencies terribly rich, but ultimately triggered a series of events that led to the loss of the companies they led and to the decline and fall of the industry they captained.

By introducing outside investors into the equation, agencies were forced to reckon with a hungry new constituency, demanding – as was their almighty dollar right – an ever-increasing return on their investment. In management's eagerness to satisfy this new group, it became more and more difficult to find the money to over serve clients, as the 15% commission system had allowed agencies to do. Inevitably, belts tightened and staffs dwindled.

The shinbone is connected to the knee bone. Clients couldn't help but notice the ebb of below-the-line services provided by their traditional agency partners and, over the course of time, went looking for them elsewhere. In searching for ways to compensate new partners, they began to question the inviolability of the 15% commission system itself. They figured that, by shaving a point or two from what they were paying their main agency, they could fund programs from a freestanding direct marketing firm or an independent sales promotion house.

The knee bone is connected to the hipbone. Once the line at hard 15 had been broken, the practice of "unbundling" gushed through the breach – creating the very antithesis of the full-service principles Stanley Resor had pioneered in the 1920s and that the J. Walter Thompson Company had championed ever since. Inevitably, agencies began to lose control of the message. Because creative ideas were coming to clients from any number of communications suppliers, the coordinating role now fell to them. The concept of sharing a long-term, institutional relationship with one agency as an equal marketing partner – to be challenged by, tussled with and mutually respected over generations – virtually disappeared.

The hipbone is connected to the backbone. Today, it is not uncommon for a major advertiser to have two or three separate agencies, a completely independent media planning and buying company, and separate resources for sales promotion and digital marketing. Because their influence on the client's overall message has been so dramatically diluted, the ready access of top agency management to the client C suite has been reduced to the occasional fly by – if that.

Nobody played the unbundling game better than Chris Clouser. He espoused a new conventional wisdom that went about like this: It's not reasonable to expect that a single communications company can be the best at everything. So, by picking and choosing from the entire universe of suppliers, a client can assemble the "best of the best" – the best advertising agency, the best media company, the best digital group, yadda, yadda, yadda.

But, in actuality, what Clouser was purposely and knowingly doing was shifting the center of advertising power to himself. As communications ringmaster, he could control a big anchor agency such as Thompson and, at the same time, throw a chunk of retail business to an old pal in Kansas City, assign the media account to a crony from New York and keep a separate creative resource at his beck and call near headquarters in Minneapolis. It was the classic ploy of divide and conquer. And while calling all to the spirit of teamwork, Clouser could enjoy the daily spectacle of group against group, engaged in fierce battle for his billing dollar.

The backbone is connected to the head bone. By losing control of so many below-the-line profit centers, big agency balance sheets inevitably became less robust, earnings suffered, and share prices eroded. This left their open books increasingly vulnerable to the likes of Martin Sorrell, who starting with JWT, began buying up the cream of advertising brands and, in so doing, paved the way for other predators to buy the rest.

The head bone is connected to the heart bone. Although these corporate raiders were successful in buying controlling interests in America's most famous advertising companies, they couldn't buy Bill Bernbach's revolutionary brilliance or David Ogilvy's haughty confidence. They couldn't buy Stanley Resor's visionary wisdom or Alex Kroll's roll-the-dice bravado. They couldn't buy Jerry Della Femina's theater of the absurd or Hal Riney's proud and provincial independence.

Before most of us realized it, the toothpaste was out of the tube. The big names that had represented deep and rich advertising cultures – such as J. Walter Thompson, Young & Rubicam, Doyle Dane Bernbach and Ogilvy & Mather – were reduced to so much JWT, Y&R, DDB and O&M alphabet soup. As each was gobbled up by soulless international conglomerates, they lost their individuality and traditional identities. And as the names lost their meanings, the halls lost their echoes.

Once agencies ceded control of the message, advertising fell victim to the tyranny of process. Now driven from the client side, the mentality shifted from "Wow, that's exciting, let's give it a try" to "We'd better run this by a bunch of housewives from Iowa to make sure we're not doing something wrong." (When asked about how much market research Apple conducted before releasing the iPad, Steve Jobs, echoing Henry Ford II from a long ago generation, said: "None. It isn't consumers' job to know what they want.") Words like "analytics" began to creep into the strategic vernacular. The game changed from seeing how large a consumer community you could gather around a big idea to chasing individual demographics across the Internet.

History will show that what heyday advertising did best was build emotional bridges between people and products. What full-service agencies did best was shepherd the message through every aspect of its development and execution; to act as steward of the brand. History will also show that, while clients may be able to make fine automobiles, handsome timepieces or fragrant underarm deodorants, they are lousy at making advertising.

You can't hardly find a good three-martini lunch anymore. And, mama, Kodak just took our Kodachrome© away.

Joe might have had it right, after all. Looking down with the perspective of years at the decline and fall of J. Walter Thompson as an independent company, a good argument could be made that Joe O'Donnell had chosen a dangerous but proper course. His discovery of financial irregularities certainly played a part in the events that led to his dismissal. But it was Joe's bedrock belief that JWT would have to go back to being a privately-held company that drove the climactic confrontation with Don Johnston and the board of directors.

"Going public had proven of no economic benefit to anybody except a few old agency guys who held a ton of stock," O'Donnell says. It didn't do clients any good. Our balance sheet was a mess. And it took agency management's eyes off of the professional side of the business."

As right-minded as Joe was about what needed to be done, his methods were interpreted by some as rash and ill considered. And that's the tragedy. If he had used a different playbook, he might have completed the cost-cutting measures he had already undertaken during his first months as president and restored health to Thompson's balance sheet. If he'd been less naïve about how business was conducted in different parts of the JWT world, he would have known when to wink and, in time, cleaned up the financial shenanigans that so offended his sensibilities. If he hadn't come across to the board as a self-serving man-in-a-hurry, he could have led the Company private with their blessing and left Martin Sorrell to hawk his shopping baskets elsewhere. Like Superman in the movie, he was JWT's last, best hope to make the earth spin the other way.

He might even have done so with Johnston's blessing. When Joe approached Don with the notion of going private, Johnston listened carefully and gave O'Donnell cautious leave to chase the possibility. "But its going to have to be your generation that leads the way," Johnston told him, too close to the end of his career to take up what promised to be a four-to-five year process. Realizing that going to the big banks and public lending institutions for funding would lead to street speculation and rumor, O'Donnell approached the Claremont Group, a private investment firm, whose CEO John Cirigliano had been a classmate of his at Columbia. As discussions deepened, the notion of Johnston remaining as executive chairman became the primary sticking point. Thompson's lackluster financial performance over the last decade gave the lenders zero confidence in Don's bottom-line leadership. Frankly, they told O'Donnell, they wouldn't lend their support as long as Johnston was in charge.

The stage was set for a contest of wills and egos between two very good men. In understanding Johnston, it is helpful to remember that he himself became CEO in a coup, unseating Dan Seymour with a carefully orchestrated plot of his devising. However, with victory, there came a measure of paranoia. Don reasoned that if he were smart enough to topple Seymour, then down the line, some young buck with another carefully orchestrated plot would be smart enough to topple him. Deservedly or not, he gained a reputation for promoting gifted executives through the ranks, and then firing them as they gained influence and authority. (Ask Wayne Fickinger, Wally O'Brien and Ron Sherman.)

As the latest gifted executive, O'Donnell spent his first days in office barnstorming the world of JWT -- kicking the tires, assessing the disparate operations and looking under rocks for evidence of evil doing. He returned with a bagful of 11 apparent acts of financial impropriety, none of which were material when considered in isolation, but nevertheless were disturbing in their pattern of loose operational behavior. Predictably, his ire was fueled by Jack Peters, who had a history of acting as the Company's Boy Scout.

Then, Irregularity #12 suddenly surfaced -- a bombshell that clearly violated foreign practices statutes and which outside counsel advised rose to the level of materiality. The law had clearly and emphatically been broken. In O'Donnell's judgment, revelation of this new impropriety might depress the value of the stock to a level where the Company could be bought with your daughter's piggy bank. A decade earlier, the Ford episode had virtually halved share price. The Marie Luisi syndication scandal knocked the stock down by half again. Irregularity #12 might have been a fatal third strike.

How many horns can a dilemma have? As the financial train was hurtling down one track, the going-private train was running along right beside. Joe was convinced that the only way the Company could get the necessary funding to go private was for Johnston to voluntarily step down as executive chairman and to accept a mostly-ceremonial non-executive chairman role – and he told him so. Well, that got Don's back up. He had not fought through decades of agency politics only to lay his sword down at this decisive moment. No, they would have to carry him out on his shield.

Trying to force Johnston's hand, O'Donnell met with Don again and informed him that he was aware of the financial irregularities and was prepared to go to the board with the story – all of it. Considering the gravity of the charges, the board would have had to seriously consider asking Johnston for his resignation. And yet, lurking way back in the nagging corner of Joe's mind was the threat of the damage the revelation of Irregularity #12 might do to the reputation of J. Walter Thompson.

Here was that dilemma again. O'Donnell was damned if he did and damned if he didn't. So, he didn't. In his presentation to the board, he left the silver bullet in his gun. He told them about the disturbing pattern of irregularities he had discovered around the world, but never mentioned #12. The board was seasoned enough to know that, even taken together, the other 11 didn't justify Johnston's removal. Don, after all, was their chosen man and, in the end, they stood firmly behind him.

Johnston had no choice but to fire his protégé and heir apparent. Right-minded as he might have been, Superman was finished, unable in the end to make the world spin the other way.

43
End Game

The call came on Christmas Eve.

"It's Clouser. I just wanted to let you know that Martin wouldn't budge on the commission deal and we fired J. Walter Thompson today. I'm going to Hawaii for a week. Call you when I get back."

I felt as if I'd been dealt a death sentence. Other than a few new business projects, I was now an Executive Without Portfolio and, at JWT, there was very little tolerance for that. If you had an account in your hip pocket, you could strip naked in the middle of Park Avenue and keep your job. If you managed a vital cog office, you could miss your stretch numbers for a couple of years and keep your job. Show up without your billing? Here's your hat.

When an agency and client part ways, it's customary to make the transition over a 90-day period. That meant we still had a substantial amount of work to do for Northwest and I set myself to doing that. But as I sat in my office, I couldn't help recall the last days of Don Johnston. Even after Martin Sorrell assumed control of the Company, he insisted that Don fulfill the last few months of his contract by coming to work at least three days a week to shuffle papers from one side of his desk to the other. In stark contrast to his former corner-office splendor, they stuck him in a dark windowless space tucked around the bend from the boardroom. When I was in town, I would sneak back to Don's cubicle for a chat (it wasn't politic, I was told, to be seen with members of the old regime). They didn't put me in a dark cubicle, but I wasn't getting many visitors either.

Clouser called with an odd request: he wanted me to be a part of his selection team for a new agency. That struck me as rather like your ex-wife asking you to help find her a new husband, but I figured "what the hell" and agreed. It proved to be an enlightening experience -- an opportunity to see how other big, successful agencies approach new business. To my surprise, they displayed an appalling sameness. Almost to a one, they spent the majority of their time talking about themselves and whatever "proprietary" system they had developed for achieving success. Every agency had a magic formula. Every team was led by a man in a blue suit who was slightly graying at the temples. They would use "case histories" as an excuse to show the best commercials they had produced for others. I watched the Northwest selection team's eyes glaze over. It was akin to being invited over to the neighbors' house on a Sunday evening to watch their home movies.

In the end, Fallon McElligott of Minneapolis won the day by not talking about themselves at all. After a brief introduction, they stood their director of strategic planning front and center and started talking about Northwest. He had no blue suit, just blue jeans and an open-collared shirt. He had no gray at his temples, but his British accent gave him a certain intellectual credibility. The utter honesty of his approach recalled eyewitness tales I'd heard of the pitch Bill Bernbach would make to new prospects. After the big agencies had marched their dozen blue suits and twelve portfolio bags in and out of the presentation room, Bernbach would go in alone and deliver a performance that became known as "one man and two easels." He would place a number of ads on the easel to his right and an equal number on the easel to his left. "This," he would say, referring to the exhibits on one easel, "is the advertising our clients were doing before coming to Doyle Dane Bernbach. And this," he said, turning to the other easel, "is the advertising they are doing now. Are there any questions?"

Evidently, out of my earshot, there were a number of conversations going on the subject of "what are we going to do with Lane?" I was a tough one. Other creative directors didn't want a former creative director hanging around. Other office managers wanted to distance themselves from somebody who had done their job. Early in the spring, I received a call from Ron Burns asking if I might stop by to see him.

"I'm afraid we're giving you notice," Burns said, after the requisite niceties, reluctant to use the word 'fired.' "We've got an office for you on the 3rd floor and you can use it for a few months, phones and all that." My time had run out.

Considering it all, I had been luckier than most; privileged to work at a profession in its prime for a Company that defined its practice. I would bet my last Clio that when aliens from a far-off galaxy land on Planet Earth, they'll discover that once upon the 20th Century, there was a powerful force called the full-service advertising agency, a marvel of art and science that mastered the craft of persuading billions of people to think and act differently; to buy

With Roger Nichols and Barry Manilow running down "Times of Your Life."

With Mike Millsap in our pipe-smoking prime. "Together, we were notorious."

Talking President Gerald Ford through a few "simple words.

Even I can be tall – especially when standing next to Paul.

That's producer Warren Aldoretta coming between me and Anka.

President and Mrs. George H.W. Bush loan us the White House for the evening.

With Kim Carnes, Steve Tubin, Michael McDonald and Paul Hoffman
during the "Sounds Like You're Right Next Door' session.

In Millimeter magazine with a story of the making of "This Old House." me, Warren,
Artie Butler, Vikki Carr and Stu Hagmann.

With Martin Sorrell during a rare civil moment.

My mother has this thing for Mozart.
All I can say is I wish Mozart had played basketball.

Kodak film.
For the times
of your life.

Sources:

This is primarily an eyewitness account. It is intended to be an anecdotal tale rather than an exhaustive historical record. To refresh and enhance my memory, I had extensive conversations with a number of the major players in the book. In several instances, I let colleagues review the chapters that involved them to which they added depth, clarity and invaluable insights.

Introduction:

A Craft, a Calling, and a Cause

II   I had read of the Bernbach/Townsend encounter in a small paperback book about advertising published in the '50s. Then, during my Ford days, I had the fortunate opportunity to sit next to Mr. Bernbach on the dais at a Detroit Advertising Club luncheon and asked him if the story was true. He retold it as reported here.

Part I:

Of Consuelo and the Dancing Man

3   About Olsen and "The American Road": *AdAge Encyclopedia of Advertising,* Ford Motor Company.

The University of Advertising

7   In 1964, *Advertising Age* published a special issue celebrating the 100th anniversary of J. Walter Thompson. I referred to and relied on this issue for basic background and historical time lines.

10   The report on Seymour's participation in *The War of the Worlds* is recounted in many places but particularly at groversmill.wordpress.com.

The Stars Align

14   In the Kodak section, much of the background material is lore, passed down to me from Granger Tripp and Alan Anderson, among others. I was introduced to Ted Geonek in 1968 when he was approaching the end of his career at Kodak. On my questioning, he elaborated this story.

15   Tom DiPaulo, a long-time veteran of the Hollywood Office confirmed the pivotal meeting with Walt Disney.

Someone Pulls a String

20   - Warner/Chappell Music, Inc. Music: Lew Spence. Lyrics: Marilyn
and   Alan Bergman.

Going Off the Reservation

25   Debussy quote: Wikiquotes.com

A Glass on the Table

34   A conversation with Mike Millsap helped recall the Norman Rockwell
          episode.

A Brand to Believe In

37   - 1973 by Paul Simon. Words and Music: Paul Simon.

Good Morning Yesterday

48   - Three Eagles Music. Music: Roger Nichols. Lyrics: Bill Lane.

This Old House

51   - Words and Music: Richard Rodgers.

52   On Kodak share of film market: *Changing Focus* by Alecia Swasy.

A Hole in the Heart

55   Andy Romano provided much of the background information on this
          ill-fated production.
56   Academy Award information provided by the Academy of Motion
          Picture Arts & Sciences

The Winds of Change

61   Sven Mohr was a great help in this section.

Too Long at the Fair

62   Gottlieb, Martin; Glanz, James (August 15, 2003). "The Blackouts of '65 and '77 Became Defining Moments in the City's History". *New York Times.*

Born and Bred -

63   Three Eagles Music. Music: Roger Nichols. Lyrics: Bill Lane.

Part II:

As in Part I, I had extensive conversations with key JWT and production people to fill in blanks and correct any inconsistencies in the narrative. I own Howie Weisbrot, Joe O'Donnell, Dick Howting, Dan Hughes, Larry Carroll and Mike Priebe many thanks for their time and contributions.

Culture Shock

71   On the strike against General Motors: Michael Barone, *U.S. News & World Report.*

72   On Northmore's discovery "Boulevard Photographic: The Art of Automo tive Advertising" by Jim Williams.

Getting Nowhere Fast

87   On Iacocca and the Pinto (from court records): "Iacocca was also the 'moving force", as one court put it, behind the Ford Pinto. In 1977, there were allegations that the Pinto's structural design allowed its fuel-tank filler neck to break off and the fuel tank to be punctured in a rear-end collision, resulting in deadly fires. Iacocca was quoted as saying "Safety doesn't sell"; he became an icon of the economic appraisal of human life. This case is a staple of engineering ethics courses as an example
of   a bad cost–benefit analysis but its complexities are often ignored for the sake of the narrative."

The Man with a Satchel

115 - J. Walter Thompson Company. Music: Paul Hoffman and Frank Floyd. Lyrics: Bill Lane.

243

Bill & Kinder's Excellent Adventure

Homage

Part III:

Steve Darland and Sherry Carniglia Paul read this section from beginning to end and offered valuable insights. In addition, I had long conversations with Rory Phoenix and Jim Sanderson about events in which they were involved. Thanks to all.

The City

Panty Palace

The 100th Monkey

Coup d'Etat

Many details of this episode came from an article by Eileen Prescott in the August 9, 1987 issue of *The New York Times* and from the Times' Philip H.Dougherty in a June 17, 1987 column.

Two if by Sea

Part IV:

A Fool's Errand

Many conversations with Denny Kuhr, Pat Rogge and Mindy Balgrosky provided detail and texture for this section.

Déjà Vu

The Camel's Nose

The View from 30,000 Feet

This chapter draws from information detailed in Eileen Prescott's 1987 article in *The New York Times*. In addition, the narrative was reviewed for accuracy by Joe O'Donnell.

246

247

249

250

Made in the USA
Middletown, DE
21 January 2021